THE CIVILIZATION OF THE AMERICAN INDIAN SERIES

Huenun Ñamku

An Araucanian Indian of the Andes Remembers the Past

Huenun Ñamku

An Araucanian Indian of the Andes Remembers the Past

BY M. INEZ HILGER

WITH THE ASSISTANCE OF MARGARET A. MONDLOCH

PREFACE BY MARGARET MEAD

NORMAN : UNIVERSITY OF OKLAHOMA PRESS

By M. Inez Hilger

Social Survey of One Hundred Fifty Chippewa Indian Families on the White Earth Reservation of Minnesota (Washington, D.C., 1939)

Chippewa Child Life and Its Cultural Background, B.A.E., *Bull. No. 146*, Vol. XIV (Washington, D.C., 1951)

Arapaho Child Life and Its Cultural Background, B.A.E., *Bull. No. 148*, Vol. XV (Washington, D.C., 1952)

Araucanian Child Life and Its Cultural Background, Smithsonian Miscellaneous Collections, Vol. 133 (Washington, D.C., 1957)

Field Guide to the Ethnological Study of Child Life (New Haven, 1960)

Huenun Ñamku: An Araucanian Indian of the Andes Remembers the Past (Norman, 1966)

THIS BOOK is printed on paper bearing the watermark of the University of Oklahoma Press and is designed for an effective life of at least three hundred years.

LIBRARY OF CONGRESS CATALOG CARD NUMBER: 66–22712

Copyright 1966 by the University of Oklahoma Press, Publishing Division of the University. Composed and printed at Norman, Oklahoma, U.S.A., by the University of Oklahoma Press. First edition.

Preface

BY MARGARET MEAD

The ethnologist sees through the eyes of others and hears with their ears. Especially when a people's life is changing and the old ways are vanishing, the ethnologist must depend for the re-creation of a world on those who are willing and able to talk vividly and accurately. Every finished ethnography is built upon such con-versations as are recorded here. But only very rarely is the reader given more than a glimpse of the process. Usually the record of the close, personal, and sometimes fragile interchange between eth-nologist and informant remains hidden away in old annotated notebooks, and only the ethnologist keeps a lively memory of an informant's personal style. Yet all this lies behind impersonal de-scriptions of how fish are caught or the sick are healed.

Sister Inez has been so concerned to present Huenun Ñamku's account as he gave it, divided as he wished to divide it among his self-selected times of coming, that she has given us also a record of how she herself works—weighing her informant's ideas gently, sav-ing his pride, matching her pace to his, bridling her scientific curios-ity, biding her time. When the proud Huenun rages at being asked something a second time, she can reassure Margaret Mondloch, her niece-assistant, that they will be able to talk with other people later. Huenun's rhythm is as valuable a comment on his culture as are the details he gives on Araucanian life.

Wisely, too, as only the most experienced ethnologist can, Sister Inez sketches in the setting in which, from day to day, she worked with Huenun. The high mountains, the schoolroom, the presence of Francisca Fraundorfner, their interpreter who knew Huenun well and had taught his children, and Huenun's horse grazing out of doors—all these are part of a living framework that slowly expands until, on their last day's meeting, they cross the fields, over and under fences, to Huenun's home and family.

This is a priceless account, one that will stand when the last Indian who knew the old ways is gone and our children's children wonder how the ethnologists of the twentieth century ever found out so much.

The American Museum of Natural History
New York City
March 10, 1966

Acknowledgments

I owe thanks to E. Adamson Hoebel, Margaret Mead, Rhoda Métraux, and W. F. and Ruth Albright for reading the manuscript of this book, for helpful suggestions, and for encouragement toward publication.

I am also indebted to my field assistant, Margaret Mondloch, to our interpreter, Francisca Fraundorfner, and the Sisters of Panguipulli Mission Station for affectionate hospitality.

To Huenun Ñamku, the informant whose conversation I have recorded in the present work, I owe most of all.

For a grant toward the publication of this book, I owe the Wenner-Gren Foundation for Anthropological Research special thanks.

For financial assistance to make the Araucanian study, I owe thanks to the Wenner-Gren Foundation, the American Philosophical Society (Penrose Funds, Grants No. 805 and No. 1341), and to my brother, the late W. P. Hilger. For a grant-in-aid toward the publication of the Araucanian study, *Araucanian Child Life and Its Cultural Background, Smithsonian Miscellaneous Collections*, Vol. 133, I am especially grateful to I. A. O'Shaughnessy of St. Paul, Minnesota.

M. Inez Hilger

St. Joseph, Minnesota
March 5, 1966

Introduction

This book is not a biography. It is not a study in ethnographical methodology, although beginning fieldworkers in ethnography may find helpful leads in it.

It is a record of Araucanian customs as related by Huenun Ñamku, an old Araucanian man in Chile. We met Huenun while making an ethnographic study of child life of his people. He lived in one of the valleys of the lower Andes near Panguipulli, a village predominantly Chilean, on Lake Panguipulli.

Of the fifty-three Araucanians interviewed, largely in their homes, during our ethnographic study, Huenun Ñamku was a volunteer informant. He, like many others, was an interested person; he wanted a truthful study made of his people. We found him to be a man who exemplified Araucanian ideals: highly intelligent, of unquestionable integrity, diligent, proud, independent, courteous, sympathetic, and warmhearted.

My field assistant, Margaret Mondloch, and I had come off the coastal range in Chile where we had spent our allotted time interviewing and observing. We were now on our way to Coñaripe, a higher valley of the Andes, where, we were told, there lived one of the least acculturated groups of Araucanians. The way to Coñaripe was a ride on a return trip up Lakes Calefquén and Panguipulli on one of the lumber-hauling boats which came down to Panguipulli from lumber camps in the Andes. The return sailing of these boats was most unpredictable. We waited in Panguipulli three weeks before we had an opportunity for a ride on one.

It was during these three weeks that Huenun Ñamku visited us at the Mission School in Panguipulli to tell us of the customs of his people. One of the teachers at the Mission School, Francisca Fraundorfner (German-born), was not only our hostess during our stay, but our interpreter as well. Huenun spoke Spanish mixed with Araucanian, a language well understood by Francisca. She had taught Araucanian children for many years, among them Huenun's children.

As an ethnographic study, this account is somewhat unusual in that Huenun was a volunteer informant. Customarily ethnographic information is obtained by interviews, by personal participation, and by observations while living among a people. Huenun's conversation recorded in this book is not found in the larger, the more complete report of our field work.[1]

Our method of ethnographic research is described in the introduction to my *Field Guide to the Ethnological Study of Child Life*.[2] A detailed description of it is also found in my essay entitled "An Ethnographic Field Method" in *Method and Perspective in Anthropology*.[3]

The Araucanians are descendants of an unconquered, aboriginal people. They opposed every invasion of the Incas (probably 1448–82) and successfully withstood for centuries Spanish and, later, Chilean attempts at conquest (1536–1883).

Today, the Araucanians of Chile live mainly on the coastal range and in the higher valleys of the Andes, in the provinces of Cautín and Valdivia. The region lies between thirty-six and forty-two degrees south latitude—the greater number of families live between thirty-nine and forty degrees. This territory extends from

[1] The latter work was published as *Araucanian Child Life and Its Cultural Background, Smithsonian Miscellaneous Collections*, Vol. 133 (Washington, D.C., 1957).

[2] Published by the Human Relations Area Files Press, New Haven, 1960.

[3] Edited by Robert Spencer and published by the University of Minnesota Press, Minneapolis, 1954.

Temuco on the north to Osorno on the south; from the Pacific Ocean on the west to the Andean watershed on the east. It is a portion of the pre-Columbian habitat of their ancestors.

The area occupied by Araucanians in Argentina today is not easily defined. The Argentine Araucanians were chased from one locality to another by the military, much as North American Indians were, and were finally subjugated by government action. They are today a conquered and subdued people. They have lost values characteristic of the Chilean Araucanians, and they are far more acculturated than are the Araucanians of Chile.

In the early days there was much communication between the Araucanians on the two sides of the Cordillera. Foot passes in use then can be traveled today. Today such passes serve as bridle paths also; one is reported as being nearly a yard deep from travel. Wider paths have served as cattle drives for years past, and serve as such today; in summer these are also used for bus and automobile transportation. Three such passes are the Tromen Pass, between Pucón, Chile, and Junín de los Andes, Argentina; another between El Arco, Chile, and Zapala, Argentina; and a third, the Vuriloche Pass, between southern Chile and Bariloche, Argentina. These passes are less than 5,000 feet above sea level; the Andes reach a height of over 22,000 feet in this region.

The Araucanian country of Chile is verdant; its climate is tempered by the Humboldt Current. The beauty of its mountain lakes and its Andean ranges, with both active and dormant volcanoes, beggars description. The height of Volcano Villarrica reaches 9,314 feet; that of Shoshuenco and of Quetropillán 7,740 feet each; Lanín, just beyond the watershed, on the Argentine side, 12,270 feet. Winter in the Araucanian country (March through October) is a rainy season. Valdivia, a coastal city in the area, reports an annual rainfall of 100 to 107 inches.

In all probability, first contacts of Araucanians with Europeans occurred about the middle of the sixteenth century. It was about that time that Spanish forces, led by Diego de Almagro, entered the Chilean Araucanian country. Almagro's forces were followed by those under Pedro de Valdivia, the conqueror of Chile. Valdivia established forts and towns within the Araucanian country. The Araucanians became apprehensive and, before long, hostile. A people not known to be exceptionally aggressive, they became fierce fighters. To their clubs and clubheads and crudely made spears and lances, they added the horse and organized cavalry— lances were merely stocks of native bamboo tipped off with arrows, but they were effective weapons. Alonso de Ercilla y Zúñiga in his historical poem, *La Araucana* (1569), praises the bravery of the powerful Araucanian war chief, Caupolicán, and the heroism of young Lautaro. The Spaniards were filled with admiration for the Araucanian fighters. In 1553, Valdivia's forces were annihilated, and he himself was killed.

During the centuries following, fierce fighting broke out sporadically. Agreements were sometimes reached, but always following them the Araucanians were treated as a conquered nation. In retaliation they burned towns established in their country by Spaniards and later by Chileans, and made surprise attacks on scattered settlements. Counter retaliation followed. Finally, in 1883 the Araucanians, convinced that it was the wisest thing to do, voluntarily conferred with the Chilean government and came to a final agreement. In this they are again a unique aboriginal people. Old men spoke to us of these days, in 1946. Quoting one of them:

In 1860 when Joaquín Pérez was president of Chile, the Araucanians were still fighting the Chileans. This type of fighting was called malón—malón is a Spanish word (a surprise attack, as by American Indians). The Mapuche (Araucanians) did great damage to Chileans: they stole animals from them, even oxen; they captured girls and women, especially girls whom they admired, and then forced these to marry them; they stole land; they destroyed small villages— they set fire to the village of Imperial twice and completely destroyed Cañete and other similar small villages. To put an end to these malones President Pérez ordered Colonel Bochef into our country. When Andrés Lienlaf, the chief cacique in our area, heard this, he set out for Valdivia (Chilean military headquarters) to speak with the Colonel. He took José Martín with him as an interpreter. . . . The Colonel treated them as traitors. José Martín defended Andrés and said that they had come to negotiate for peace and not for war. The Colonel had received orders to exterminate all Araucanians from Valdivia northward to the province of Arauco. To convince the Colonel of his good will, Andrés got on his knees and took an oath that he would tell all Mapuche under him that they must put an end to these malones. The Colonel then gave him three months of grace. Andrés was to return to the Mapuche and tell them to end their attacks. Andrés returned. He talked to the caciques. Some would not agree with him; they said that he had turned traitor to his people and land. . . . Later the Colonel came here to sign the peace with the cacique, Andrés. He disembarked at Chan Chan with 1,500 soldiers. When we saw him lead these soldiers on to our land, our people fled and hid; they thought that now their homes would be burned and they themselves exterminated. The women wailed. But this ended the wars. That is how the Mapuche in this area saved themselves from annihilation.[4]

It seems more accurate to say that since 1883 there has been infiltration and penetration by Chileans into the Araucanian country, rather than that the Araucanians, because of subjugation or submission to the Chilean government, are being forced into acculturation.

Written accounts call these people Araucanians, a word probably derived from the name of the *araucaria* (*Araucaria araucana* or *Dombeya Chilensis*), a tree that grows in the area—Araucanians call the tree *pewen* (or *pehuen*). The Araucanians call themselves *Mapuches* (people of the land). History, however, records the *Mapuches* as only a division of the Araucanians, other divisions being *Pehuenches* (or *Pewenche*) of the Andean Highlands (people living where the *pewen* or *pehuen* grows), *Picunches* (people in the north), and *Huilliches* (people in the south). According to present-day Araucanians, the terms *Pehuenche, Picunche,* and *Huilliche* are used by them only when speaking of *Mapuches* living in the particu-

---

[4] *Araucanian Child Life and Its Cultural Background, Smithsonian Miscellaneous Collections,* Vol. 133 (Washington, D.C., 1957), 3–4.

lar area referred to; among themselves, in all areas, they speak of themselves and of all the others as *Mapuches*. While living among them, we found this to be true.

Araucanians are unique, too, in the language they speak. Their language is classified as an independent linguistic family and is called Araucanian.[5]

Culturally the Araucanians of Chile are a sedentary, agricultural people; they were this when the Spaniards first met them. Today, in all areas, they also breed cattle and sheep. For those living on the coastal range, fishing and shellfish gathering in the Pacific have always been a means of subsistence. Lakes supply fish for those living in the Andean valleys. For the Chilean Araucanians trapping played a role, but not hunting. In pre-Spanish days the Argentine Araucanians were hunters, principally of guanacos (*Lama guanicoe*), rheas (*Rhea americana albescens*), pumas (*Felis concolor*), and armadillos (*Chaetophractus villosus*). Today, they are chiefly small breeders of cattle, horses, and sheep, and, on a lesser scale, they are horticulturalists and agriculturalists.

The total population of Araucanians is not known. Depending on the source consulted, those in Chile number 97,000 to 150,000 persons. Estimates by early Spaniards ranged from 500,000 to three times that number.

The Araucanians of Chile expect members of their families to have stamina, self-respect, courage, and to be law-abiding. Formerly, families were polygynous; today, they are mostly monogamous. Although attendance at state or private schools is compulsory in Chile and most Araucanian parents see to it that their children attend school, they do not hesitate to voice their conviction that the responsibility for education of their children is theirs. Training children in the mores of the people is part of the total education of the child, they insist, and parents, consequently, make it their duty to train them in these, as well as in their native language. Oratory is held in high esteem; boys are trained in it. Grandparents do not function in the capacity of teachers unless they are rearing a parent-

[5] *B.A.E. Bulletin 143* (1946), II, 695.

less child. There is no induction into the tribe, nor are there puberty rites for boys or girls.

The Araucanians have a well-developed sacrificial religious ritual. All attend its performance. Christian Araucanians, however, in general are merely observers.

The early government of the Araucanians was rudimentary, but effective. All fathers of families had a voice in it. Caciques had limited jurisdiction, but their powers were well defined and were respected. In time of war they elected as a leader the most aggressive cacique; his power for the duration of war was almost unlimited. Changes are now going on in the Araucanian way of governing. Encroachments of the Chilean government are noticeable everywhere. Caciques have been deprived by the Chilean government of most of their rights and responsibilities. Their former duties as judges are now largely in the hands of Chilean courts, and resident rural Chilean policemen enforce Chilean laws. Araucanians expressed concern about these changes while we lived with them in 1946–47 and 1951–52. They seem defenseless toward action that is being taken by the central government of Chile which is intended to nullify Araucanian claims to lands which have been theirs for centuries, claims based on tribal customs and decisions; they believed their claims were rights secured to them at the time of final pacification by the Chilean government. "Here we are, back again in the days of 1883: broken promises! And our leaders have no longer the rights guaranteed them by agreement," said Huenun Ñamku. There is submission on the part of the Araucanians only in matters where resistance is futile. There is resistance, but to no avail, to payment of taxes on land, to compulsory education, to curtailing of activities by shamans, and to enforcement of laws by resident rural Chilean police instead of caciques.

Araucanians are hospitable among themselves and toward strangers. Willingness to help can be relied on. Both men and women take an interest in their personal appearance. Special friendships exist and find expression in a ceremonial. Praising an individual's intelligence is the finest compliment that can be paid an Arau-

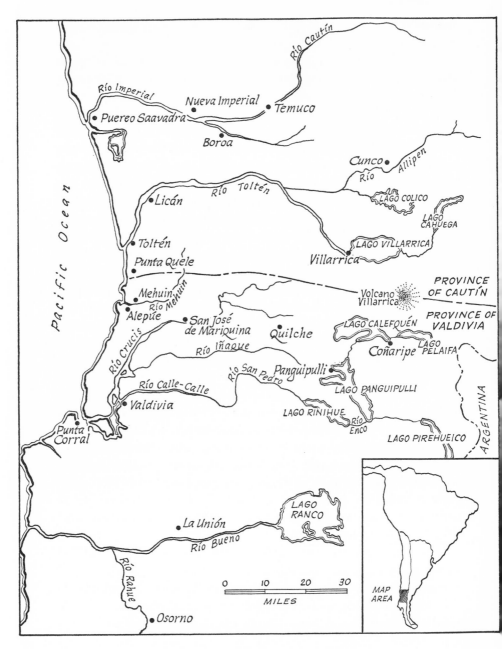

ARAUCANIAN COUNTRY OF CHILE

canian; he is deeply hurt by expressions of disdain for his intelligence. Patience is an accomplishment, especially on the part of women. In general, women, both young and married, live chaste lives; in general, too, men show respect for women. Leisure time is spent playing a form of hockey and other competitive games. Wrestling and swimming are pastimes also.

The father of a family demands obedience from children and wife—or wives, in case of polygyny. Occasionally, quarreling between husband and wife occurs; when it is prolonged, the wife not infrequently relieves the situation by hanging herself. Murders, too, occur, but not often. According to Chilean policemen on duty in the Araucanian country, Araucanians are law-abiding citizens. Such arrests as are made usually result from theft or from injury inflicted on a non-Araucanian during a drunken brawl.

Chicha, here fermented apple cider, is the intoxicating drink today. Araucanians admit that its introduction has resulted in a deterioration in their people and that drinking to excess has become a vice. In pre-Spanish days *mudai* was the alcoholic beverage. It took time and much human effort to produce it: women spent days chewing corn or grain and spitting it into an olla, where it took more days to ferment into *mudai*. There was only enough of it for all men to drink of it to intoxication on special occasions. Two such occasions were the end of harvest time and after the erection of a dwelling. To this age-old custom that men drink to excess on these specific occasions there have now been added the days of Chilean fiestas. In pre-Spanish days, *mudai* was the beverage at meals, also; today it is drunk only at the tribal religious ceremonial, but never then to excess.

In the event of sickness, herbalists and shamans are called on. The cause of all sickness is the ill will of another; it is inflicted by witches. Ill will may also result in witchcraft being exercised on those one loves or on one's fields, crops, and cattle. It is expedient, therefore, to have the good will of everyone.

In their aboriginal culture the Araucanians were a self-sustained people with a well-integrated way of life.

We found, while we lived among them in Chile, that much of their aboriginal culture is still intact, especially on the coastal range and in the higher valleys of the Andes. But even these areas can be characterized as moving slowly toward a Chilean-Araucanian culture. The culture of the lower valleys and of the great central plain of Chile has made decided advancement in this direction. Acculturation is due in part, no doubt, to the compulsory education laws of Chile, which oblige all children, including Araucanians, to attend school; to encroachment of the Chilean government on rights and claims to land ownership; and to advantages sought by Araucanians in economies provided by Chilean cattle dealers and Chilean-Argentine lumber companies that operate in the Araucanian country.

Contents

Illustrations

MAP

Huenun Ñamku

An Araucanian Indian of the Andes Remembers the Past

CHAPTER I

Huenun Ñamku, Fisherman and Trapper

Huenun Ñamku (pronounced "hwēnūn' ny'äm' kū") arrived in a huff this morning. He shook hands with us, but perfunctorily, not heartily as when we first met. No comments were made about the weather. No pleasantries were exchanged. We knew that there was a storm raging in Huenun's head. He began: "Some young *Mapuches* [Araucanians] scolded me last evening for giving you information about our ways and our old customs. You are probably laughing at me, they said, because I tell you about them; that you will most certainly laugh at me when I bring you that model cradleboard that I promised to make for you."

Then in a defiant, determined manner he pulled a chair up to the table where we were sitting, and at which we had interviewed him on a previous day, sat down, and went right on: "But I decided that it was because some *Mapuches* in the past had not told the truth about us that those senseless and incomprehensible things have been written about us. I have heard what some of them are. I want the truth told about our people. I am not only ready to help—that is why I am here—but I offer to go with you to Coñaripe, or to any other place where there are *Mapuches*. I will see to it that you will meet intelligent persons there who can give you correct information and who will tell the truth about us. I am interested in seeing the book you will write about our people not only completed but above all one that will tell the truth. I agree with you: it is important that a record be made of our way of thinking and our way of doing things; future generations of *Mapuches* should know what kind of people we were and what our customs were. I know that our way of doing things is even now changing. Look out that window. Do you see that Chilean cutting his grain? He is doing it with a combine; he cuts and threshes that grain with that one machine. If you go with me to the other side of that hill, you will see a *Mapuche* family there cutting its field of grain with sickles. Next week you will see them threshing that grain by having horses tramp on its ears. The people will lay the grain on the ground in a fenced-in enclosure—we call it *lila*—so that ears lie within the range of the horses' feet as they move around and around in the *lila*. Horses will tramp for hours on those ears. Things are changing for us. In due time, the *Mapuches* too will be using combines."

All this Huenun said in a tone of voice and in a manner that bespoke determination and conviction. He seemed to be in deep thought now. Soon he added, "I want you to say in that book that you are writing—and in a prominent place—that *I* gave you information."

Margaret Mondloch, my field assistant, wished that those young *Mapuches* had heard Huenun utter that last sentence and had seen his face as he said it. I said to her, "If Grandpa Terres"—my Grandpa Terres was her Great-grandpa Terres—"if Grandpa Terres had spoken that last sentence, he would have sealed it with certainty by bouncing his fist on this table." This was our second interview with Huenun. Our first interview had taken place two days before.

Margaret and I had come off the Chilean coastal range, had crossed the great central plain of Chile, and were now in Panguipulli valley on Lake Panguipulli, one of the picturesque lakes in the lower ranges of the Andes. Huenun Ñamku lived in this valley. Margaret and I had spent nearly two months on the coastal range living with and talking to Araucanians. (Huenun calls his people *Mapuches*; ethnologists call them Araucanians.) We had made notations of what we had been told there by Araucanians about their way of

4

living and also of what we had observed. We had interviewed in their homes most of the families living on the coastal range.

The least acculturated Araucanians on the coastal range we reached by riding to them on horseback, the only means of getting to them. Those living in the Andean valleys, we were told, could be reached on horseback if we followed old trails around the lakes, in this case Lakes Panguipulli and Calefquén, or by water if we sailed across the lakes. Small, wood-fueled, steam-propelled boats, known as *vapórs* (pronounced "vä pôr'"), sailed across them, each ferrying an open freight boat, known as *lancho* (pronounced "län' chō"), loaded with lumber. The *lancho* is hitched to the side of the *vapór*. The lumber is portaged from a higher lake to a lower one by trucks or oxcarts.

Margaret and I had come to Panguipulli to get a ride to Coñaripe on a *vapór*. Our plans were to stay in Panguipulli just long enough to arrange for transportation to Coñaripe. The sailing of the *vapórs*, we had been told, was most unpredictable: sometimes, two or three sailed in one week; at other times, one sailed only every two or three weeks.

Upon our arrival in Panguipulli, we heard that a *lancho* was being unloaded. Francisca Fraundorfner, one of the teachers at the Mission School in Panguipulli, went with us to the pier to find out when this *vapór* would leave for its return trip up Lake Panguipulli. The captain had no idea when his *vapór* would sail; he would let us know; and he promised to take us with him.

Upon our return to the Mission School, we met Father Sigifredo, a German Capuchin priest who had spent more than fifty years among the Araucanians. He spoke their language well; he knew all the areas in which Araucanians lived; he knew most of the Araucanians by name. He had notified Huenun that we were arriving in Panguipulli this day. Huenun had heard some weeks before that we were in the Araucanian country collecting information, said Father Sigifredo, and that we planned to write a book about his people. Huenun wanted to be notified of the day of our arrival; he wished to meet us and help us.

5

Before we returned from the pier, Huenun had arrived. He was waiting for us in the classroom that Francisca had prepared for our use. The classrooms were vacant, for it was summer vacation. She had shoved some desks toward one wall and others toward the opposite wall. Between them she had placed a long table for our use. Father Sigifredo took us to the classroom, introduced us to Huenun, and left for his office.

As we entered the classroom, Huenun was looking at some pamphlets and my Chippewa and Arapaho studies, materials we had brought with us and which I used to introduce informants to what we planned to do with the information we were collecting. It was a way, too, of arousing their interest, of motivating them, and of letting them know our objective. "After all," I would say, showing an informant the books, "people in our parts of the world have had their customs recorded, and now the children of their children's children will know what the customs of their own people once were." I would then ask, "Do you think that your people would find it interesting to have their customs recorded so that the children of their children's children will know what your customs were?"

Huenun pointed at the word "primitive" in the title of one of the pamphlets—he recognized the word because of its similarity to its Spanish equivalent, *primitivo*—and asked with that authoritative air, compounded of importance and responsibility that we soon learned was characteristic of him, "Are you going to use the word 'primitive' in the title of your book on the *Mapuches*?"

I answered, "Do you think we should?"

Promptly he replied, "Most certainly not! Most certainly not! That word can be used when speaking of less intelligent people than the *Mapuches*, people like those in the islands of the Pacific, the Easter Islanders, for example; but not when speaking of the *Mapuches*. When our young men returned from the war [World War II], they told us of the customs of the Pacific islanders. *These people are primitives*, I can assure you! Then, too, do not let us use the word 'Indians' anywhere in the book. The *Mapuches* are not Indians." He pointed at the word "Indians" in the title of another

6

pamphlet. We had already been instructed by Bishop Guido Beck, vicar apostolic of the Araucanian country, before beginning our field work, not to use the word "Indians" when talking to the Araucanians; the word is offensive to them. It connotes servitude and subjection, for it was first heard during the days of attempted subjugation by the Spaniards who invaded their country.

Huenun now stood there; he was studying us. He glanced at Margaret, then at me. "So you two have come here from North America to learn our customs." We took a good look at him. His face was serious. His eyebrows formed shelters for his dark, intelligent, penetrating eyes. His wrinkles were deep; they furrowed his weather-beaten face. His mustache hung beyond the corners of his mouth. (Occasionally, men on the coastal range also had mustaches, but no beards, something I had not seen among the North American Indians.) His hair, he must have thought, was in place—he had just run his fingers through it to put it there. He wore shoes and had a hat, signs to his fellow Araucanians and to others who knew as much—we had learned this on the coastal range—that he had means beyond the immediate necessities of life.

I said to him, "You are a man of many years, Huenun; you must know a great many things that we should like to know. How old are you?"

He replied: "I think I am eighty years old. I have reckoned this to be my age because I was told by our old people that I was still tied to my cradleboard when the *Mapuches* from across the Cordillera—from what is now called Argentina—not only chased our people back here, but pursued them into our country. Our people had gone over there to rustle cattle, something they often did; but never before had they been pursued. From this event I reckon that I must be eighty years old, but the truth is I do not know how old I am. But who wants to know that? Of what importance is that for your book? Last August, I wanted to go to Argentina on a visit. I had to go to Valdivia to get a permit to leave Chile. There they wanted to know the date of my birth. I fabricated a date for them, and also for other facts about myself. I said that I was born on August 30, 1889; that I had been in military service in 1903; that I was married on May 7, 1907. Of what importance can it be for anyone to know all this about me?"

Huenun was still interested in our books and pamphlets. He picked them up, walked to the other side of the table, and sat down. He examined them some more, and then remarked: "I want to tell you another thing about your book. Do not put the picture of a *Mapuche* woman on the cover of it; that is most certainly not the place for the picture of a woman; the picture of a man would do all right." He was referring, we learned later, to the picture of an Araucanian woman on the cover of *Lecturas Araucanas*, a book published in 1934 by Félix José de Augusta and Sigifredo de Fraunhäusl, the Father Sigifredo whom we had just met.

"How about putting *your* picture on the cover?" I ventured.

"You could always be satisfied then that you had an intelligent, representative *Mapuche* on it," he answered, and laughed heartily. He continued, "I once saw a book that an Argentine fisherman had—he was around here fishing in our lakes. The cover of that book pictured a trap for catching four-footed animals; I think it was a trap used in a faraway country. You might photograph one of our traps and use it on the cover of your book."

"What sort of traps do the *Mapuches* use?" I asked.

He took a scrap of paper and made a sketch. "This is a trap for catching fish in a stream," he said. "It is a circular one, and we call it *llolle*. Men use it in catching large, lively fish." And he went on to describe its making: Men lay down *colihüe* (*Chusquea culeou*, native bamboo) stalks, side by side, with the slimmer ends in one direction—stalks must be two arm-spreads in length; they must not be shorter. They are tied into position with a stout vine, using an over-under weaving technique. When tied, the whole has a fanlike shape. The sides are now brought together and fastened to each other, giving the trap the appearance of an elongated frustum. Huenun noted that the diameter at XX may be any width, but at X it must never be greater than a single hand-spread; if it is greater, fish turn around and swim out again at XX. Before the trap is set,

8

large branches of trees are planted rather closely together along the trail indicated by *y*'s. "This is like a fence," said Huenun; "we call it *müko*. To some branches about the middle of the *müko*, we fasten the trap so it will stay in position. The fish come into the *müko*, then look around to find another way to get downstream, and find this way to be into the *llolle*. Here they swim out at *X* where a man stands ready to grab them. I have made *llolles* and fished with them; we fish with them at night. Large fish, as you know, come downstream in schools, two or three times during a night."

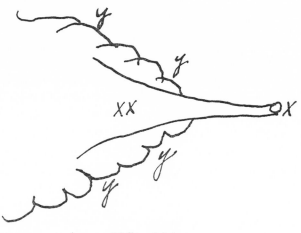

Llolle, a fish trap.

Before going into the stream to fish, Huenun went on to say, each man makes a fish stringer for himself. He finds slightly curled vine and takes three pieces of it, each about an arm's stretch in length. He ties these together, using one to make a knot about the middle. "A stringer looks like this," he said, and sketched one. "In *Mapuche* we call it *mauche challwa*." The men are ready now to fish. All walk into the stream. Each takes his turn at *X* of the *llolle*. When a fish comes through, the man at *X* catches it with his hands, pokes an end of a vine of his stringer through the gills, and pushes the fish toward the knot. The catch is carried home by grasp-

9

ing the knot. "No, no, fish cannot slide off! How could they? The vine is curled."

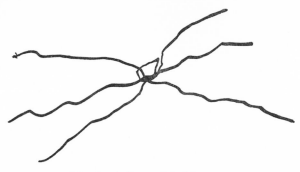

Mauche challwa, a fish stringer.

Women and children, Huenun went on to say, catch less lively fish than do men. One of these, a favorite, is the *puyen* (*Galaxia maculatus*), called *upesh* in Araucanian. Women catch these in a long basket-like trap called *chiñe*, which they weave with the technique used in weaving a *chaiwe*, that is, a household sieve that serves as filter and for draining. While making the sketch of the *chiñe*, he remarked, "*Upesh* are found in certain small rivers and in brooks. *Upesh* come in schools; they are rather tame. One can see their backs as they come downstream. Women know where to find them. When the women see them come, they walk quietly into the stream. Before long you can see the women chasing back and forth, scooping up *upesh* with their *chiñe*. I saw them fishing in this manner in the creek at Baihuenta recently."

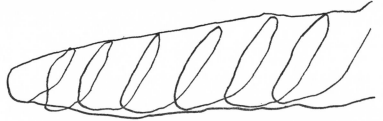

Chiñe, a fish trap used by women.

10

Huenun had not heard of anesthetizing fish by spilling into a stream decoctions made of specific plants. My question, however, reminded him of something women do that either tranquilize fish or put them on the alert—he did not know which. One woman in a group ties a snake to a fine strand of horse sinew and leads it slowly upstream from the very mouth of the stream; the other women walk upstream also, at the same pace as the woman leading the snake, but do so on the bank. "That snake," continued Huenun, "seems to tame fish, for fish coming downstream turn around and move slowly back upstream. When they come to a shallow place with a sandy bottom, they collect in schools. Here the women on the bank can easily see them; in reality, they do not have to look for them, for the *wala* [a water bird, not identified] sees them before the women do and gives the women notice of them. He stands near the school and calls '*Waa-waa-waa-waa.*' The women step off the bank without speaking, walk slowly and quietly to where the *wala* indicates that the fish are, and then gaily scoop them up with their *chiñe.*"

Men also spear fish from the banks of streams. Huenun had made a spear by hollowing out a *colihüe* stalk, except a handstretch at one end. He sliced this end into halves lengthwise, sprawled the halves, and inserted between them two additional splits of *colihüe* of the same length. To keep these four splits apart, he fastened twisted sections of stout vine between each two. Such a spear is called *nülewe*.

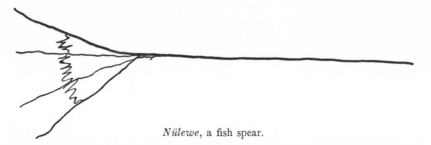

Nülewe, a fish spear.

Five kinds of fish were caught in Andean streams by Huenun. He gave us their Araucanian names, and we identified them by their Spanish names and classified them. They are *lipügn* (Perca; *Percichthys trucha*), *peliolo* or *peloilla* (*peladilla; Haplochiton taeniatus*), *kauke* or *remü* (*pejerry; Patagonia hatcheri* or *Atherinichthys argentinensis*), *upesh*, and *fosha*. We were unable to identify the *fosha*. Huenun described it as a fish without scales, with few bones and a large head that had two soft horns. He sketched a *fosha*, but destroyed it when he could not decide whether the horns turned forward or backward. "We eat *foshas* only when food is scarce and other fish do not come our way," he added. "When we have come to this, that fish no longer come our way, we sacrifice the blood of a lamb or of a sheep on the bank of the stream in which we intend to fish. We kill the animal and sprinkle its blood heavenward while we say a prayer of petition to *Chau* [God]." He tried to give an exact translation of the prayer, but found it difficult. It is a prayer, he said, asking God to bless the people with a much-needed haul of fish. The meat of the lamb or sheep is taken home by those men in the group who made the sacrifice.

Huenun went on to say that *kaukes* are extinct. He laid the blame on the Canadian salmon with which Andean lakes had been stocked in recent years. "These salmon, I fear, have devoured the last one of them," he said regretfully. "Even now you can see salmon swimming out of lakes and up and down our streams looking for *kaukes.*" His concern about native fish reminded us of the concern we heard expressed by non-Araucanians who also fear that before long all native fish in Andean lakes will be extinct; all lakes are being stocked with foreign fish, they told us, because the Chilean lake region has become a foreign fisherman's paradise. Huenun continued: "*Kaukes* vary in size: some are two hand-stretches long, some only one. *Kaukes* are caught in the spring. Young men make a sport of catching them—they catch them by hand from banks of streams. When I was a young man, we went to a brook or small stream where we knew there were *kaukes*; we went there after sunset and built a fire on one of the banks. While the fire was getting a good start, we each got ourselves several *colihüe* stalks, or maybe several dried branches of maqui [*Aristotelia macqui*]. We laid the

12

end of each in the fire, and as soon as it was in flames, we sneaked back to the water, swished the burning end over the edge of the stream a few times, and then held it there very still. Before long various fish came swimming lazily toward the light to see what it was. When we spied a *kauke*, we reached quietly into the water, grabbed it at its underside near the head, and dropped it into our *wallka*. Every man had a *wallka*, that is, a pouch suspended from his neck by means of a strap. But those days seem to be gone forever," Huenun said somewhat saddened.

It was now "coffee" time. Francisca brought hot tea made of dried raspberry leaves, a *Kaffee-kuchen* topped with eggs and raw sugar, and some jam made of wild-rose hips. After refreshments, Huenun went out to talk a little to his horse. He led it into a better grazing spot and hobbled it there. He returned, and continued: "And now I want to tell you how we trap wild animals. Puma [*Felis concolor*], *mara* [Patagonian hare; *Dolichotis patagonia*], in fact all four-footed animals, we trap in a *wachi*. When I was young, there were many of all of these animals around here. *Wachis* can be of various sizes—the size depends on the animal to be trapped. It takes three men to set a large one, the kind used to trap a puma. Here is how such a one is set." He then described, with the aid of gestures, the setting of a *wachi*. A sapling of *avellano* (*Gevuina avellana*), three to four arm-stretches in length and four times the measure from tip of thumb to its first knuckle in diameter, is needed. It is placed an arm-stretch deep in the ground in a slanting position. (An *avellano* sapling is best because it has more spring than any other sapling.) One end of a long, twisted horsehair rope is fastened to the upper end of the sapling; the other end is tied into a noose. Because of the slanting position of the sapling and the weight of the rope, the noose is brought to rest at a short distance from the base of the sapling. The bait, usually raw meat, is placed in the noose and fastened to it. Next, by some ingenious arrangement, a vertical pole supports two horizontal ones. These three poles keep the *avellano* sapling in a bent and taut position, and this sets the trap. No tying is done anywhere. And now the men go home.

13

Sooner or later a puma comes along. He gets at the bait, and while eating it, he pulls it; consequently, the three poles collapse. Their collapse releases the sapling; the sapling springs into position, and, in so doing, it contracts the noose about the puma, usually about his neck; soon the puma hangs in mid-air. "And that is how a *wachi* works."

Huenun continued: "There was a time when a puma could be expected at any time of day, anywhere. Today they sneak out of their lairs only at night. They look for sheep from which to suck blood. It is for this reason that we corral our sheep at sundown. If a puma's footprints are seen around a place two successive mornings or if the blood of some sheep has been sucked by him, we have to build a trap to catch him. This trap differs from the *wachi*, but it is an old *Mapuche* type also; it never fails to trap the puma. It is built to protect the sheep, but for certain to catch the puma!" He drew a diagram and pointed out that the trap is a circular enclosure with a narrow entrance, which is in reality a blind alley; it is a trifle larger than the body width of a puma, but much longer than his body. In building it, stout saplings are planted solidly in the

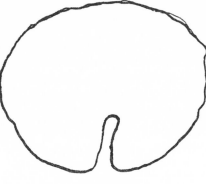

Puma trap.

ground leaning slightly outward. Their leaning position prevents the puma from jumping over them into the enclosure. The saplings are held in position by intertwining vines, two rows at the bottom and two at the top. Any open space that may show up around the bottom after the intertwining is done will be so well plugged with sticks and brush that the puma cannot push his way into the enclosure. However, here and there between the saplings, spots will be thinned out, so that the puma can see the sheep inside. "I have seen a puma walk round and round and round such an enclosure snuffing every time he caught a glimpse of the sheep," said Huenun in a whisper, extending his nostrils and snuffing, too. "Finally, he finds what looks to him like an entrance, and sneaks into it. A puma is smart, but man can outwit him. Once in the gangway that he supposes to be an entrance, he finds he is in a narrow, blind alley, one much longer than his body. Once in it, he cannot turn himself around; he must back out. When he does so, a man who has been on the lookout stabs him with a lance. Our family owned such a lance; we bought it from a relative who made them. He made them of iron and silver coins that he had got trading with persons other than *Mapuches*.

"I was told that my father-in-law's wife stabbed a puma—generally women do not stab animals. It happened when my father-in-law's wife and another woman were in the *ruka* [dwelling] alone. The other woman collapsed from fright when she saw the puma, but my mother-in-law went out and stabbed the puma just as he was backing out of the trap. She had thrust the lance into his heart. I myself have never trapped a puma in this manner; my grandfather did. I saw him set up such a trap; in fact, he trapped seven pumas in this way. And now I must tell you how we trap and snare birds, and after that I must go home."

Birds are trapped by a ladder-like affair made by tying saplings together. Huenun had used vines to tie the parts. Such a ladder is generally two arm-stretches in length and one in width. When set as a trap, one end rests on the ground at an angle greater than forty-five degrees and is bolstered in that position with a pole. One end of a rope made of twisted horsehair is tied to the middle of the pole, while the other is held by the trapper, who sits very quietly a short distance away. Directly under the ladder seeds of wild grasses

15

and/or wheat are piled in a heap; toward the edges they are scattered haphazardly and sparsely to entice the birds. When several birds are feeding under the ladder, the man jerks the rope, thereby releasing the ladder and trapping the birds under it. "Are the birds killed, or only stunned?" I asked.

"Killed! Most certainly killed!" said Huenun. "The ladder is heavy!"

We had seen little Araucanian girls trap pigeons in a similar manner, but the pigeons were only stunned; however, the girls had used a window screen in place of a ladder. We all had pigeons for supper that day.

To snare birds, Huenun said, a man makes a noose in one end of a thin horsehair rope and lays the noose on the ground. To hold it in position, he places a piece of wood or a rock just above the running knot. Seeds are placed inside the noose to serve as bait. Next, tall sticks are set in the ground in a circle around the noose, with an opening left at the knot. Since a bird can neither land on the sticks nor fly directly into the noose, it will walk through the opening and land at once in it. The snarer, who has been sitting a short distance away holding the other end of the rope, pulls the rope and closes the noose about the bird's legs when it is getting seed.

I then asked Huenun how the pùdu, a small reddish deer (*Pudu pudu* or *Cervus humilis*), and the armadillo—Araucanians call it "peludo" (*Euphractus sexcinctus*)—are caught. He answered: "At one time, pùdus were plentiful in our country; today, there are very few of them; occasionally one sees footprints of one—they look like the footprints of sheep, but much smaller. Pùdus have not been hunted in my lifetime. And I have never seen a peludo. Does the peludo have feet? Four feet, you say? Oh yes, now I know: it is the animal that rolls itself up when attacked, or burrows a hole in the ground, scratching so much dirt between the layers on its back that no one can pull it out of its hole. I have been told that there are many peludos on the Argentine side of the Cordillera. But I know nothing about catching them. And now I

16

must leave for home. Darkness falls fast in these mountains. Do you wish me to come again?"

I had hoped Huenun would ask to return, for I believed we had in him an independent thinker and a reliable, intelligent informant. Margaret was of the same opinion. I answered, "If you can come here every other day, Huenun, we shall stay in Panguipulli for a while. I am not given to flattery, but I do want to say to you that I find you to be an intelligent and reliable man."

He replied more than promptly, "I thank you for that compliment. And I want to tell you that when Father Sigifredo introduced you, I at once recognized that you had enough intelligence to know that I had some. I shall be here at nine o'clock in the morning, the day after tomorrow."

This completed our first interview with Huenun. Margaret wrote in her notebook, "Today's interview ended as a mutual admiration party!"

Huenun did not think that he should be paid for the information he had given us. He agreed, however, that payment such as he would receive if he were working on a *fundo*—a farm owned by a Chilean—would be fair. We paid him accordingly in Chilean money. Later we discovered that material things, especially food, were more acceptable than cash. He bade us *adiós*, and was on his way home.

17

CHAPTER II

Transcribing Field Notes

If at all feasible, Margaret and I would spend the day following an interview transposing the notes that we had taken the previous day—on this particular day we transcribed our notes on fishing and hunting. I had learned from prior field experience that there was an advantage in doing this as soon as possible. If we wanted to record an interview with ethnographic notations describing the psychological reaction of the informant, it was necessary to do so while we remembered the interview. Reactions, such as moods or emotional displays, are often culturally rooted or closely associated with the personality of the informant. Since we had also learned while transcribing earlier notes that the interpreter could, at times, be helpful, we arranged to have Francisca with us or at least nearby. Sometimes she was able to settle disputes arising from details of a note; sometimes she clarified a note that neither Margaret nor I had understood clearly; often she contributed from her own experience something that she was reminded of because of our questions or by what the informant had told us; often she stimulated new questions because of her interest in what we were doing.

Francisca sat near us, knitting; she was ready to help us if we should need her. It was a joy to have her with us in any event: she was jovial and gifted with common sense. She knew Huenun well, and she had taught his children. Although she admired his intelligence and "stick-to-itiveness," she said that she would find it an ordeal to refrain from putting Huenun in his place if ever he displayed his temper; she knew that he would put on an exhibition if ever his pride was hurt. "He is like all the *Mapuches*," she added, "as proud as any human can possibly be." Since she and I had agreed that the duty of a good interpreter was to interpret only, she consented to being a "good" interpreter. During nearly all of our subsequent interviews with Huenun, Francisca interpreted for us, but when it was impossible for her to do so, one of the sisters, also a teacher at the Mission School, substituted for her.

When transcribing a note, Margaret would read it to me from her shorthand notebook. (Much of her shorthand was actually long-hand with abbreviations and improvised characters, with Araucanian words and Huenun's sketches and diagrams interspersed.) Francisca and I would discuss the note to make certain that it was what Huenun had said and that it was accurate in every way. I would then dictate the wording of the note, and Margaret would write it, in her customary manner, on paper measuring four by six inches. Margaret headed each paper with the informant's name—in this case, Huenun's—with the informant's age, his habitat, and the date of the interview. We gave a title to a note to indicate what information was recorded on it. If we disagreed, Margaret would write the note as I dictated it, but she would indicate our disagreement by placing a check mark over the title of the note. After we had labeled notes in this manner, we would try to clear them with the same informant at our next interview or, if that was not possible, with a subsequent informant.

We had now completed the transcription of our first interview; Margaret indicated this by "X-ing" out the pages of her notebook. With Francisca still with us, we agreed on topics to discuss during our next interview with Huenun. Also, we had decided that we ought to clear up certain details regarding the information he had given us on fishing and trapping on which we differed. Some information collected on the coastal range we had classified as "doubtful"; we might check this with Huenun. We had other information collected on the coastal range labeled "incomplete"; it needed to be completed. We still had many topics about which we had no information at all. And then there was the intriguing area of comparative information. Our plans for our next interview were now ready. Francisca dropped her knitting and attended to her other duties. Margaret and I relaxed. We again agreed that Huenun was a good informant and that we should stay in Panguipulli for a while since he seemed eager to help. I said to Margaret, "I shall be greatly mistaken if Huenun does not come prepared tomorrow to tell us what *he* thinks ought to go into our book."

It was late afternoon by now. Margaret and I took a walk to the village of Panguipulli, in which mostly Chileans live. Children playing marbles along the road abandoned their game to skip along with us. Mothers came to chat across fences that enclosed their gardens and homes and yards—fences built of volcanic rubble or blackberry brambles. Accompanied by the children, we visited small shops—generally each was only a room on the street side of the home—and bought cookies for each child. As we walked home, we heard a vendor on the street cry, "Watermelons from the country of the *Picunche*," which was quickly followed by the price. We walked up to him, selected several melons, and asked him to deliver them to the Mission School. He did so later, and we paid him his price.

Mothers living along the path which led back to the mission handed us small bunches of radishes, carrots, onions, and other garden vegetables to show their good will.

We spent the evening with the sisters and Francisca, sitting in a large room in bright moonlight, visiting, and listening to German songs which they had sung in their beloved fatherland and which I had often heard my father sing. Several sisters had not yet heard from their families in Europe although World War II had ended months ago; they hoped that their families had survived the struggle. We said our evening prayers with them and retired. I wondered if Huenun would be back in the morning.

CHAPTER III

Ruka Building and Food Preparation

I t was morning and time for Huenun to arrive. While we were waiting for him, Margaret went to the kitchen to fetch embers— the morning was cool. She had surmised that there must be plenty of embers in the kitchen stove which had been used to bake bread for our breakfast. On the coastal range we had invariably started our fires with embers. Even the Araucanians there shared embers with each other from their open fireplaces. On the coastal range, evenings and days when the winds blew in from the Pacific were cold. The sisters there had improvised a "heater" for us: glowing charcoal placed on top of sand that nearly filled a large pail. We were grateful for the warmth that radiated from the smoldering charcoal. The rim of the pail was Margaret's foot warmer. Here, in Panguipulli, we were to get warmth from a small potbellied heater which thoughtful Francisca had set up in the classroom. "The mornings in the Cordillera are cold, and so are the hours of the early forenoon," she said while she heaped kindling on one pile near the stove and short pieces of wood on another. "So are the evenings always cold, and the afternoons, too, once the sun has gone behind the Cordillera. You will need a fire most of the day in order to be comfortable; we want you to enjoy your days in Panguipulli." I expressed concern because I thought the stovepipe, which was routed out through the upper pane of a nearby window, ended too close to the wall. Francisca took a look and assured us there was no danger of fire.

21

Margaret was returning with a hearth shovel, full of glowing embers. "Here they are," she announced. "I knew that wherever that yummy bread was baked there must be embers! And Huenun has arrived. I saw him hobble his horse." Soon we heard him walking through the hallway that led to the classroom, his spurs tapping the floor at every step. I had noticed that each spur was merely a thong with a serrated wheel of heavy tin fastened to it.

This is the morning on which Huenun came in a huff. After he had had his say about those young Araucanian fellows who had chided him for giving us information about the customs of his people, he began: "Last evening a relative stopped at my *ruka* [dwelling] to ask me to help him build a new *ruka* for his family. In the Panguipulli area you will find few *rukas* like those in which all *Mapuches* lived when I was a child, that is, the ones made of a framework of saplings and completely overlaid, roof and walls, with thatch. But in Coñaripe you will find many. In Panguipulli, today, we build our *rukas* mostly of slabs of lumber that we get at the lumber mills in the mountains. These mills are owned by Chilean-Argentine lumber companies. Some mills give us slabs when we ask for them, provided we have a team of oxen to drag the slabs away at once; other mills ask us to pay for the slabs by working with our teams of oxen at the mills for a few days.

"I shall now tell you how we build a thatched *ruka*. Today, too, I want to tell you about our food customs. When I told my wife that I had told you about the *Mapuche* ways of fishing and trapping, she said she saw no sense in that unless I also told you how fish and meat were prepared as food; so I shall also tell you about our foods. But first of all I want to tell you how we erect a thatched *ruka*." Huenun had come prepared to lead the interview!

Rukas, he said, are usually built when the *copihue* (*Lapageria rosea*) are blossoming. The man who wishes to erect a thatched *ruka* goes into the woods and finds saplings of *pellín*, that is, saplings of any tree that has a hard core—the Chilean oak (*roble chileno* or *roble pellín*; *Nothofague obliqua*) is one. Since the saplings are to form the framework of the walls, each must have a

22

crotch. The best saplings for rafters and tie beams are those of the *ulmo* (*Eucryphia cordifolia*); they not only are hard wood, but grow straight. The man also brings home stalks of *colihüe*, the bamboo-like plant.

When the man has gathered the materials for the framework, he tells ten to twenty men the day on which his *ruka* is to be erected and invites them to come. These men are usually neighbors and others whom he himself has helped to erect a *ruka*. Men who are relatives bring their families and food.

On the day designated for the *ruka* building, two men are appointed to supervise the work and each selects an assistant. "We call the supervisor '*kafu*' and the assistant '*inkafu*,'" Huenun explained. Half of the men are assigned to each *kafu*, and take orders from him. Generally, each *kafu* feels responsible for erecting half of the *ruka*; however, all men work together until the *ruka* is completed.

Several men, probably five from each group, are sent to fetch *ratonera* (*Hierochloe utriculata*)—a grass used for thatching—from grassy fields, usually pastureland. Huenun recalled instances when the wives of a man had gathered the *ratonera* on the day preceding the erection of a *ruka*, but he did not think that this was work for women. "Each plant must be pulled out with its roots—stems without roots are useless—and pulling these is hard work," he added. "Anyway, it is easier to work with *ratonera* when it is green and moist; day-old *ratonera* is already drying."

Other men are assigned to strip the leaves and twigs off the *colihüe* stalks; still others begin to erect the framework of walls by setting young *pellin* saplings firmly into the ground some distance from each other. When this is done, a line of *colihüe* stalks is tied horizontally to them, two to four hand-stretches above the ground. About four hand-stretches above this line another line of *colihüe* stalks is fastened; there may also be a third and a fourth line, depending on the height of the *pellin*. All tying is done with vines.

While the framework for the walls is being erected by some men, others tie saplings together for rafters and tie beams. As each rafter is completed, it is lifted and set into the crotches of two opposite saplings of the side walls, and is securely tied there. When all rafters are in place, the vertex of each is tied to a ridge pole. Lines of *colihüe* stalks, probably two or three, are now tied to the rafters in horizontal position, beginning with the eaves, about four hand-stretches apart. This completes the framework.

Thatching begins with the roof. Bunches of *ratonera*, with roots earthward, are spread out on the *colihüe* stalks at the eaves and, by a twining technique, are tied to each other and to the rafters and *colihüe* stalks beneath them. To keep the *ratonera* from shifting position, a line of *colihüe* stalks is placed over it horizontally, a handstretch from the eaves, and tied to the rafters from underneath. A second row of *ratonera* is now placed so that it overlaps the first, and is fastened into position in the same manner as the first row. Successive rows are so placed and fastened until the roof is completely covered with *ratonera*. Huenun made certain that we understood that the roots of all *ratonera* must be earthward and that every layer must overlap the one beneath it. He said, "If you are careless about this, your roof will not shed the rain properly: you will have rain coming in here and here and there and there. I am telling you how to build a *ruka* as it should be built."

Next, the walls are thatched in the same manner as the roof. A thatched *ruka* has one or two entrances, but it has no windows or chimney. Smoke is emitted through openings left in the walls at gable ends and/or through a section of *ratonera* left thin in one wall, the choice of the wall depending on prevailing winds. The floor is the bare earth. "At night and in cold weather these floors are always warm. Our fireplaces—they are really holes in the earth—are never without glowing embers or a fire, and these warm the floor of the *ruka*," added Huenun.

By the time the *ruka* is completed—building it may take the greater part of the day—the women are ready to serve a plentiful meal of barbecued mutton and toasted wheat, a repast which is part of the *ruka*-building event, as are certain playful performances and excessive drinking. Huenun described these activities. After the

24

Huenun Ñamku, "High Flying Eagle."

Maríañuke, Huenun's wife, wearing the traditional Araucanian dress and silver jewelry.

Vapór *with* lancho *on Lake Panguipulli.*

The village, lake, and valley of Panguipulli.
Note the snow-capped peak of the extinct Volcano Shoshuenco.

Young Araucaria tree.

Eruption of Volcano Villarrica in 1949.

Mature, nut-bearing Araucaria tree.

Father Sigifredo, a German Capuchin priest who had
spent more than fifty years among the Araucanians
of the Andes. Father Sigifredo arranged for
the author to meet Huenun Ñamku.

ruka is finished, the two *inkafus* come forward and make a great pretense of fighting each other. Then they go away to prepare for the performance. Each makes himself a mask by cutting openings for eyes and mouth in a piece of an old poncho, which is kept in position by a woven band tied about the head. At the end of a string attached to the mask is a whistle made from a section of a sheep's leg bone. Each *inkafu*, as he makes his appearance, holds a drum under his arm; he can, however, suspend it from his shoulder with a strap. The drum is made from a hollowed-out section of tree trunk with the ends covered with a horsehide kept taut by a thong laced through holes cut along the edges of the hide. Feathers of rhea, canela leaves, and *copihue* flowers decorate the drum. Huenun repeated that *rukas* are usually built when the *copihues* are in blossom.

Each *inkafu* beats a rhythm on his drum with a drumstick and blows the same rhythm from his whistle. Huenun pantomimed holding the drumstick in one hand and the whistle in the other. Everyone sings. "Here is the song we sing," he said, as he handed me the paper on which he had written it. He sang it in Araucanian: *"Ayünnellulai reihue ruka tu ülmen, kuche mañagua, nerkeofun knoafun, taüpupülli ruka, antu mañagua, nerkeafun kona. Fun taüpupülli ruka, chalilmeaufinüui, señoria piñone, kaita ulmen, en mai pen."* He translated it: *"This empty* ruka *of the man, now rich, is very beautiful. If I had all the things of the moon for this* ruka, *on this earth below, and if I had all the things of the sun for it, they would all go into this* ruka *on this earth here below, as a gift to the women of this man who is now rich."*

After this song everyone settles down to eat to satiety of the barbecued mutton and toasted wheat. Following the meal, all men drink chicha, beyond satiety. "That is our custom. Some drink so much that they are not yet sober on the following day," declared Huenun. "And the man who does not drink to complete intoxication on such an occasion as *ruka* building is not a real man." Margaret told him that she did not think that there was a *real* man there in that case. He looked at Margaret with that piercing look of his

25

and pulled his bushy eyebrows forward—he was always intrigued with what Margaret had to say—"She seldom talks," he said, "but when she does, it is significant."

We now took time out for our midday meal. Huenun's dessert was watermelon. "Every Araucanian enjoys watermelons. Huenun will be delighted with these," said Francisca as she placed them before him. Margaret and I enjoyed a dessert of shiny, luscious, wild blackberries, sweetened with raw sugar. We had cream and home-baked bread. Our beverage was tea made from the leaves of wild roses. After we had eaten, Huenun took his siesta on the grass near his grazing horse. When his siesta ended, we went back to work.

Huenun began: "And now I want to tell you about some of our food habits. A favorite food is *funa poñü*. Chileans like it, too, but they call it *papa funa*—both terms mean 'fermented potatoes.' " He went on to say that on a day in the fall of the year, as soon as potatoes are fully matured, the men of a family go out to find a place in which to ferment the family's supply of potatoes. They look for a spot near a somewhat rapidly flowing brook, but not too rapid. They divert the water at this place and dig a hole. A cubical hole will do, but Huenun preferred a cylindrical one with a depth equal to its diameter. The size of the hole depends on the quantity of potatoes the family wishes to ferment. Huenun had fermented as many as three sackfuls at the same time. The bottom and sides of the hole are densely lined with layers of large-leafed ferns—these grow in all moist places in the Araucanian country—or with leaves of maqui (*Aristotelia maqui*). Fern and maqui are preferred because they transmit no taste to the potatoes as other plants do. Huenun himself preferred ferns, for with them he could cover every bit of earth space, something difficult to do with maqui leaves.

Potatoes, washed clean of all earth, are dropped into the hole until it is completely filled. The tubers are then covered with a thick layer of ferns or maqui, and all is weighted down with stones as heavy as a man can carry. The stones, too, are washed clean so that no taste of earth or manure might penetrate the potatoes.

The brook is now permitted to resume its normal flow, but in such a way that the water flows over the hole. "Stay until you see the water coming up between the ferns and flowing off, for then you will know that every potato is in water and that the scum which rises to the top will be carried off. Now you may go home, but occasionally go to see if the water is still flowing. After the same phase of the moon as the one when you put the potatoes into the hole has come and gone twice, it is time to dig up a potato or two to see how the fermenting has progressed. The potatoes are ready for eating when they are decidedly floury and no longer watery. They may, however, be left under water for another moon. When they are ready to eat, we say they are *chuño* or *lip poñü*; they are delicious then." Non-Araucanians said that fermented potatoes were vile smelling and held their noses when merely speaking of them. Fermented potatoes are removed from the hole as needed, but with caution, for rough handling causes them to fall apart. Before they are taken home, they are washed clean of slime and earth, if earth has collected on them. For regular meals they are boiled in clear water, but if a delicacy is desired, they are boiled in sweetened or salted water. Sweetened or salted potatoes are left lying around in the *ruka*, and anyone feeling hungry eats some. "*Funa poñü* is an old, old *Mapuche* way of preparing potatoes," commented Huenun. "Chileans who prepare them in this way have learned it from *Mapuches*."

Formerly, honey of wild bees was used for sweetening, but today both honey and sugar are used. Huenun recalled hearing old people say, when he was still a child, that before bees were introduced into the area, there was no way of sweetening food. Children at that time sought sweetness found in the nests of *yiullíñ* (a species of hornets), which could be found near rotted tree roots or fallen, rotted tree trunks. "We would find these nests and suck the sweetness from them. I myself often did this. We would watch the *yiullíñ* to see where it would fly after collecting sweetness from blossoms. Later in the season we entertained ourselves by quietly sitting close to a nest watching the *yiullíñ* sting those big flies that come then. These flies tried to get some sweetness, too. A fly would whirl round

27

and round to mislead the *yiulliñ*, but the *yiulliñ* would finally sting it, and the sting of *yiulliñs* is mean. So, the poor fly would leave with a sting, but no honey!

"However, when I was a boy, we already collected honey from the hives of wild bees; they had their hives in hollow trees. My grandfather said that the bees must have come to our country from some other country. When we needed honey, we searched for a hollow tree on which bees were crawling in and out; we knew that honey would be found there. We built a fire near the tree to drive the bees away with smoke; the smoke did not kill the bees, but it did bewilder them and keep them away while we took the honey. Once the bees had left, we cut down the tree and took the honey from the trunk. The bees would find themselves another hollow tree in which to deposit their honey and would only return to their old hive to reclaim the honey we had not stolen."

Salt was obtained from places across the Cordillera where it was known to collect on the earth's surface. "We went there on horseback," said Huenun. "Every man took several pack horses with him to bring back a supply."

It was getting late, and I knew Huenun would soon have to leave for home. He had not yet told us how to prepare fish and meat as food. I thought his wife would be pleased to hear that he had done so, and I wanted to lead him into telling it, but Francisca advised against it. "He will interpret it as though you were reflecting on his ability to do a good job. Let him go on, otherwise his pride will be hurt!"

He went on to say that another staple food in his boyhood days was wild grain, that it grew in abundance in his country, but has now been replaced by domesticated grain, mostly wheat. "I would like to bring you samples of those wild grains, but I do not know where to find any; around here cattle have eradicated them with their grazing; maybe you will see some in Coñaripe. Since I have never heard these wild grains called by any Chilean names, I do not think that the Chileans used them as food. [We, too, classified as borrowed culture traits those for which we found no native

28

word.] As a boy, I helped my grandmother pluck the ears off the stalks and thresh them with our feet—we thresh our wheat in this way today when our stored supply is exhausted before the new crop has been threshed. We spread the ears of wild grain on hard ground in the sun, and at night we dance on them to a song that everyone sings. Children so high [his gesture indicated they were probably nine or ten years old] are allowed to dance; I often did so as a child. Everyone dances in turn until he is tired. We sing: *'Beat, my feet. You and the jilguero, break these ribs.'* The *jilguero* is a bird. And we dance like this [he shuffled his feet two steps forward, three steps backward, and then took a long step forward].

"My wife grinds wheat into flour today, as women have always done, on a metate using a muller," added Huenun. Huenun, however, had the larger portion of his wheat ground at one of two flour mills in Panguipulli village. He went on to say, "Each old woman owns a metate; young women can, on occasion, be seen searching for metates in the shallow waters of the Thawal, a river that flows through Trakapulli. Stones shaped like metates come down that river." He thought that water action had shaped them and that there was nothing mysterious about it.

Speaking of metates made him think of several that had been excavated in the woods nearby while Chileans had been digging in the area. They found pottery, potsherds, metates, and mullers, said Huenun. Metates and mullers were shaped exactly like the ones used by his people today, but the pottery and potsherds were very different. "People must have lived here before the trees grew into these great forests, for how else could these things be found deep down in the ground, much lower than the roots of these trees," he reasoned. "Has anyone told you that people lived here before the *Mapuches* did?" he asked. We had seen prehistoric pottery in the home of a Chilean of German descent in San José de Mariquina, a Chilean village in the Araucanian country.

Speaking of pottery reminded Huenun of dishes used when he was a child: wooden dishes, wooden spoons, and cups made of horn. "One seldom sees a wooden dish today," he said, "but spoons and

29

cups of horn can be seen in many *rukas*." He had helped his uncle make cups and spoons from horn, and he proceeded to tell about it. As soon as an ox died, his uncle extracted the horns, including their roots, and cleaned them thoroughly. If it was cups he wanted to make, he cut off the tip end of a horn and discarded it; the remainder he cut into pieces of desired lengths, the length of each depending on the size of the cup he wanted to make. Usually no more than three cups could be made from one horn. The narrower end of each piece was plugged with a cork of wood. (We saw cups of horn used as measuring units in village stores. Liquids, such as oil, and dried foods, such as beans and peas, were being measured in them.) If spoons were needed, his uncle boiled a horn in water or buried it in ashes in the fireplace, very close to the fire, until it was pliable. He flattened it then and carved spoons of various sizes from it. Huenun had seen only steel knives used for cutting. "I have often tried to find out from our old people what was formerly used to cut up a puma, or any animal, for that matter," he said, "but no one seems to remember."

He went on to tell how his people toasted wheat. Formerly, a *lupe*, a specialized piece of pottery, was used. The *lupe* was set up in a slanting position, wheat was put into it, and hot ashes added. The wheat and ashes were stirred with two wooden spoons. The wheat, as it toasted, became lighter than the sand, and because of the tilted position of the *lupe*, it fell out free of sand. Today, wheat is toasted in open pans over an open fire, usually out-of-doors, and is continuously stirred to keep it from scorching. We saw children at school toasting it in this way.

Huenun continued: "I have told you how we fish, and now I want to tell you how we prepare fish for eating. I shall not have time to tell you how we prepare meat; it is late. But there is not much to tell about it, anyway. One way is to twirl strips of meat around a pole or rod—it looks like a screw when on the pole—and hold it over the open fire until roasted. It takes two persons to roast it in this way: one holds one end of the rod, and the other holds the

30

other end. Both keep turning the pole so as to roast the meat on all sides." (A true barbecue, thought Margaret.) "Sometimes" added Huenun, "women cut the meat into small pieces and cook these as a stew in an olla. It is left to the women to decide how to prepare meat for a particular meal.

"But I want to tell you how we prepare fish. Let us say that several men have just caught some *kaukes*, and that each has as many as he needs. Each man slits the bellies of his mess, removes the entrails, and washes out the cavities. At home heads are severed and skins stripped off. The woman decides how she will prepare the fish: she may cook them in an olla with a little salt, or she may roast them." If they are to be roasted, the woman rubs the visceral lining with a mixture of salt and chili (*Capsicum annuum*) and then either places the fish directly on hot coals in the fireplace or pokes sticks through their backs and holds them directly over the flames. Fish are eaten only when well done, but fish eggs are eaten raw.

Huenun continued: "Now, it may happen that men decide to roast fish while they are fishing—sometimes they are hungry because they have not had a complete meal that day. Formerly, we had one substantial meal between sunrise and sunset, and it was eaten whenever all the food was ready. Anyone hungry at bedtime ate left-overs." He then returned to the fish: "Each man then prepares a fish or two in the manner I just told you, that is, he pokes a stick through the back of each and plants each stick in a slanting position close to a fire. The men continue to fish, but keep an eye on the ones being broiled. As soon as they notice the heads and skins falling off, they know the fish are ready to eat." Huenun had not heard that his people baked fish by rolling them into large leaves, burying them, and then building a fire over them. We had met young Chileans, vacationing along brooks, who were doing this.

Huenun had seen men start fires with fire drills. To start a fire in this manner, a man sliced a section of a *colihüe* stalk into halves, put one half on the ground, flat side down, bored a groove at its middle point, and in the groove, using both hands, rotated the

31

stalk of a rosebush. The lower end of the rosebush stalk is rounded, and its length must be ten times that from the tip of his thumb to his first knuckle. If it is longer or shorter than this, the friction will not be sufficient to produce sparks. The *colihüe* stalk may be of any length. Fungus found on trunks of the *coihüe* (*Nothofagus dombeyi*) is best as tinder; it is placed close to the point of friction.

Old persons had told Huenun that formerly there were years when the earth did not produce enough staple foods to feed the people. "I heard very old people say that at such times some *Mapuches* lost their minds from hunger and ate the flesh of those who had already died of starvation. But usually the earth produces some foods that can be eaten. People can eat, if they must, cooked dehydrated flowers of *notro* [*Embothrium coccineum*] and *alverjana* [*Vicia nigricans*] and powdered stems of the large fern. The core of rotted *colihüe* can also be eaten. About every fifty years," he added, "we have a year of hunger. There is one due soon, it is prophesied; the newspapers say the same, and those who receive knowledge in dreams agree; the *huincas* [non-Araucanians] also say so. But truly, we have not had a year of plenty for a long, long time. I think we should conduct a *gnillatun* soon—*gnillatun* is our religious ceremonial. If we do not, we shall have years worse than the one that is predicted. In reality, bad years have already begun: Insects, which come here from the north, are already eating the roots of wheat. Worse than the insect is the *gorgojo*, a worm that eats the very heart of wheat kernels. Another kind of worm, a black one, is eating our garden produce. We must conduct a *gnillatun*! Although I am now a Christian, I still have much faith in our own religion, and I want to be responsible for conducting the *gnillatun* just once more." He sat quietly as though thinking faraway thoughts. "And that is all for today," he said sadly.

We presented him with a number of watermelons this day. He was greatly pleased with them and said they were the best pay we could have given him—his wife and children would be pleased when they saw them. He tried to hide them in his saddle bags to surprise them, but he had to carry two large melons with him on his saddle.

32

"Tomorrow I shall help my relative build his *ruka,* and the next day I shall be back here. *Hasta luego! Adiós!*" he called as he rode through the gate.

"*Adiós,* Huenun! *Adiós!*"

CHAPTER IV

Traditions, Songs, and Riddles

It was three o'clock in the afternoon, and Huenun had not yet arrived. Since he had not failed to come at the time agreed upon for our previous interviews, I began to think that he had decided to come no more. Margaret thought that maybe those young *Mapuches* had influenced him and that we would not see him again. We began to talk of moving into the higher valleys of the Andes where the least acculturated Araucanians live.

The notes in Margaret's notebook had been transcribed, and those that needed checking were so indicated and were properly sorted into packs. We wrote one additional note, one on the *koyaqtun*. The *koyaqtun* is a formal expression of courtesy extended by Araucanians upon their arrival in a home or when accidentally meeting someone on the road. Francisca and the sisters at the Mission School had made certain that we knew how to perform it, for we needed to know the acceptable and proper manner of meeting Araucanians, they said. We had been given the same advice by the sisters on the coastal range. To me the *koyaqtun* was important as the proper manner of making contacts.

There were two things, Francisca told us, that we should never omit, for omitting them was a direct insult and an almost unforgivable act of discourtesy. The first was to shake hands with every man, woman, and child, including swaddled babies, who came to see us or whom we met on the way or whom we found in a *ruka* upon our arrival. The second was never to omit the *koyaqtun*. Between

Huenun and us the *koyaqtun* was carried out about like this: We shook hands. Huenun asked, "How have you been?" I answered him. He asked, "How is your family in North America?" I answered. "How are the people in your country?" I answered to the best of my knowledge. "How are the indigenous people there?" I answered this—made a fair guess, in any event. "How are the sisters here with whom you are staying?" I answered again.

Now it was my turn. "How have you been, *Señor* Huenun?" He answered. "How is your family?" He answered. "And how are your relatives?" He answered. And so we continued. Then he turned to Margaret—he had already shaken hands with her—and asked her nearly the same questions he had asked me. She answered each one. However, since she had heard my questions and his answers regarding himself and his family, and since hers would be no different, it was not expected that she ask him to repeat for her the information regarding his people. This *koyaqtun* was performed upon Huenun's arrival.

The performance of the *koyaqtun* having been recorded as a last note, we ate dinner. After our siesta we had *Kaffee* and *Butterbrot* with marmalade. Then we settled down to formulate our plans for moving to Coñaripe. After all, it was there that Bishop Buido Beck had told us that we would find old customs intact. He had spent nearly fifty years among the Araucanians and knew all the areas in which they lived. According to the map, our route to Coñaripe led across Lake Panguipulli and then over a stretch of land along the foot of Volcano Shoshuenco to Calefquén. Calefquén appeared to be a village. From there, it seemed, we could either cross Lake Calefquén by *vapór* or skirt the lake by oxcart or possibly on a lumber-hauling truck—there seemed to be a road indicated as well as an oxcart trail. We had been told that a *vapór* ferrying an empty *lancho* sailed for lumber almost daily from Calefquén to Coñaripe. We had also been told that there was another mission school at Calefquén and that the sisters there would house us and tell us the best way to proceed. We decided to discuss our plans with Father Sigifredo. He had told us that he would get word to the

35

sisters in both Calefquén and Coñaripe of the approximate day of our arrival in each place after we had set the day on which we would leave Panguipulli.

Just as we had decided to do this, in walked Huenun. He was more than a little tipsy. He was in high glee. "Prepare to take more information," he called to us. I turned to Margaret and said, "This information, Maggie, will be remarkable!" The word "remarkable" was a cue to her at all times, in any sentence that I uttered, that I doubted the correctness of the information—it was a cue for her to precede any notes she made with a question mark. The question mark gave us notice when transcribing that the information had to be verified. She now knew that all the information given us by Huenun on this day should be verified.

Well, here he was! Here was Huenun. Too much chicha! The *ruka* had been built, and the day had ended as all days end when a *ruka* is built—with a chicha spree, a spree that lasted as long as there was chicha, sometimes through the night and into the next day. He volunteered information immediately. There was no need of leading him. After relating a number of amusing incidents of the *ruka*-building day, he told of one man—one who had also assisted in erecting the *ruka*—whose mode of dress was so antiquated that he was still wearing a chiripa, the traditional pants worn by men—an oblong piece of home-woven cloth known as *chamall*. "He was a picture of the ancient times—that man was! You would have seen an old custom, if you had seen him!" And he shook with laughter, shaking his head back and forth. "And here is how a chiripa is worn." Up from his shoulders and over his head came his poncho. "You will have to use your imaginations now and think of this poncho as *chamall*. I must apologize to you for not using *chamall*, but only this poncho; but then, women weave ponchos and *chamalls* much alike." At this point he shook hands with us, saying he had forgotten to do so, and apologized. He obviously forgot the *koyaqtun*.

"As tipsy as he is," Margaret said in an undertone, "he does not forget his courtesies." Handshaking over with, he placed one of the

36

long sides of his poncho around himself, a little above the waistline, folded its ends over each other in front, and said, "Now I should secure it here [at the waistline] with a *chamallwe* [belt]; but I have none." He walked to a desk where our boxes and books rested, his poncho trailing after him like a train, took a cord and said, "I'll use this cord instead." He then pulled the lower end of the poncho forward from behind between his legs, brought it to the waistline, and tucked it under the cord. "There now! That is all that there is to a chiripa. Sometimes a cacique wore a *chamall* and let it hang down like a skirt, but more often he wore it in chiripa fashion. My grandfather never wore pants like we do today; he wore a chiripa until his death; in fact, he died in one. That is exactly what he died in! The chiripa came to us from Argentina. Maybe that is why some of our caciques never wore *chamall* like a chiripa, but wore it like a skirt. In Argentina men have to do much horseback riding, and a man finds it easier to ride in a chiripa than in a skirtlike *chamall*. One thing has never changed for *Mapuche* men: all *Mapuche* men have always worn a poncho."

Part of Huenun's afternoon performance consisted of singing songs in Araucanian. He told about each song, sang it, and translated it. "Before a man sings this one," he said, "he tells how it originated. And this is what he says: A man is resting on the ground. He falls asleep and dreams that he sees a bird high in the sky. The bird circles around, then swoops toward him and says to him, 'Circle around a few more times with your horse, uncle *kalkin*.' It tells of spreading news by signaling with fire and by maneuverings done by men on horseback." He then explained that the *kalkin*, the *mañke* (condor), and the *ñamku* (eagle) are three important birds—in fact, they are the most important birds—and that they are really related to each other and are good friends. *Kalkin* is the oldest; he is the uncle of *ñamku* and *mañke*. *Kalkin* is an important bird in Argentina, also. "In fact," he went on to say, "I have heard that he is the most important one there. And now I shall sing the song. It is really one sung by the Argentine *Mapuches*. Here is the song [he wrote it in both Araucanian and Spanish in Margaret's notebook and then sang it in Araucanian]:

37

Why will you not open up and let me fly to get the news, my ñamku? *See, fire is creeping along on the heights of the Cordillera. On the foothills there is also a fire burning. What news can that be? What news can it be,* mañke? *News? You will go to* kalkin, *your uncle, the one that lives one day from here on the top of the rocks. Then you will know the news: the news that the fire is telling. Would that you would make a few more circles with your horse. Oh, our uncle* kalkin!

"And now I shall sing two songs as sung by *Mapuches* on our side of the Cordillera," said Huenun. He translated each. His first song:

Up on the hill, in the middle of the hill, flies my ñamku. *What news will he tell me, this my* ñamku? *He circles fast with his horse. Up on the hill, in the middle of the hill, my* ñamku, *my* ñamku. *Come with some news. Up on the hill, in the middle of the hill. He comes to make a fire. Yes, up on the hill, in the middle of the hill. What news will this be that* ñamku *brings me?*

His second song:

Our kalkin *lives. Listen! The* mañke *sits upon the rocks on his domain. He knows that news will come. They come to make a fire up on the hill, in the middle of the hill, so that* kalkin *will see it; he, the only one that is living up there, our* kalkin. *Listen! He sits up there on the peak of that rock—that is his domain—in order that his horse will bring news, news that comes with a fire, up in the mountains. And so the news comes to* kalkin.

Another song as sung by Argentine Araucanians followed:

I made my horse run, nephew, the old low bred. He stumbled to the left, like an ordinary horse. They come, they come, those from the south. [He interjected, "They are the *Huilliches.*"] *They come, they come, they bring news of the fire. They come to burn. I have a small son, old enough to come on a horse by himself. Come, I give you whatever you ask: if you wish a piece of* chamall *or a fine head covering, I will give it to you."*

At this point I asked him if his wife ever sang songs. "She?"

38

And Huenun chuckled. "She sings to herself when she works at home, but [with some disdain] I never listen to her singing." He then sang a song in Spanish which Araucanian women sing as a pastime—one learned from Chileans. He explained that it told of a woman who ignored a man, named Vincente. The man had come to ask her parents to let her marry him. The man went away disappointed. He then worked hard to forget his sorrow and accumulated possessions. She lived in poverty. Later she composed the song. Huenun said, "I shall now sing it: *'Let us go to this place,' so said Vincente. 'In this place we shall be happy. There we shall be respected and make ourselves representative human beings.'* [He explained that this meant that they would have property there.] *So said Vincente. 'I closed my heart against him then, and now I have great grief on this earth. But if I go to Vincente, I shall be happy.'* One person or many can sing this song. Whoever wants to learn any song can do so by singing with others who sing it." He went right on: "And here is a song in *Mapuche,* one sung by a young man who wants to marry a girl: *'I tell you sister, we would be happy if we were married.'* And that is all that this song says. There is not much sentiment expressed in it."

Following this I asked him to tell us an Araucanian riddle. "Here is one," he responded promptly. "I see something. Guess what it is?" The answer was "A eucalyptus tree." He could see one through a window. "Here is another: What am I thinking of?" The answer was "That it might rain."

Since he did not seem to grasp the meaning of the word "riddle," I said, "I shall give you one, Huenun, one that was in a German reader we used at school when I was a child. Here it is: *"Panz in Panz, sieben Bein, und einen Schwantz. Was ist es?"* (Francisca translated it into Spanish. In English it reads: "Belly in belly, seven legs, and one tail. What is it?")

He laughed loud, in fact so heartily that tears rolled down his cheeks. "Whatever it is," he said, "it ought to have another leg!" The answer is "A cat in a three-legged kettle."

He had caught on now. "The *Mapuches* have no riddles," he

39

said. "Chileans do. Here is one that I heard a Chilean man ask: 'What goes out of a house and does not come back in?' The answer is 'Smoke.' "

The sun was about to sink behind the Cordillera. We urged him to start for home. A bag of yerba maté (Paraguay tea) was his pay this day. We invited him to return another day. "Tomorrow I cannot come, but I shall be back the day after tomorrow. Jerónimo, my son, is sick. The herbalist who is treating him wants some of the medicinal water found on a *fundo*, and I must go to the *fundo* to get it. *Adios! Adios!*"

"*Adios!* Huenun! May God be with you, and take you home safely!" I replied. Margaret and I looked at each other. We were adding to our profile of Huenun.

CHAPTER V

Curative Knowledge and Practices

This morning Huenun arrived before the appointed time. Since the sun was not shining, he had guessed at the time of day. He seemed embarrassed, but made no reference to his conduct of two days ago. However, he did apologize for scratches on his face and on one of his ears and then looked at himself in a mirror, a small one that fitted into the palm of his hand. He explained that he had fallen into a bush of brambles and added that he wished the scratches were not there.

"How is Jerónimo?" I asked as a last question of the *koyaqtun*.

"Better," he answered. "I fetched the medicinal water the herbalist wanted; I brought home four large bottles of it, all that my saddlebags would hold. The *inquilinos* there [tenants on the *fundo*] are very strict. They have put up a sign that reads, 'No trespassing.' I knew from this that I had to get their permission to pass through fences on the *fundo* to go where the water is. I had to do much explaining before they let me go through. The water is in a pool and tastes and smells of sulphur. The herbalist boiled certain herbs in it and applied the decoction to Jerónimo's carbuncle. It gave him relief. One of the *inquilinos* told me that people can drink the water from this particular pool, and I found the water to be cold. However, there are many pools in the Cordillera which are exceedingly hot. Sick *Mapuches* sometimes bathe in these waters; so do Chileans. Near Lake Pelaifa, at a place called Maligue, there are four pools of green, slimy water, one lower than the other; each lower one cooler than the one above it. If you go higher still, you come to Carringi, a place near Reihueco, where the water is so hot that one can cook food in it."

Huenun, emptying his pockets of medicinal plants, now said: "I collected some of these on the *fundo* yesterday on my way to the pool and some on my way from home this morning." He had a number of complete plants, but only roots or leaves or flowers of others. "All of these," he began, as he spread them across the table, "have curative values. There are many more plants around here that have medicinal value and that are used by our people, but I know only the values and uses of certain ones, and these are some of them." He held up one plant: "This is *kimwe* [not identified]. A decoction of the entire plant cures all stomach ailments except pain in the stomach. For pain in the stomach we swallow a mixture of powdered *paico* root [Chenopodium ambrosioides] and powdered chicken-gizzard lining. For wound infections we heat these leaves [*culul*; not identified] over a fire and apply them directly to the wound.

"And now here are some remedies for sore eyes: If your vision is blurred, if it seems as though a cloud were in the way, scrape this *welke* root [*Solanum valdiviense*] well of its rind and all dirt, extract its sap and that of these *lanko kachu* leaves [*Bromus unioloides*], mix them with saliva, and wash the eyes with it—you can extract the sap best by rubbing the leaves between the palms of your hands. However, if an eye is sore because it was scratched by a twig or got a blow of the hand, put mother's milk into it: if the eye is a man's or a boy's, then the milk must come from a mother nursing a girl; if the eye is a woman's or a girl's, the milk must come from a mother nursing a boy. If you do not know what makes the eye sore, apply a decoction of this plant, called *küñalfillkun* [*polipodio*; *Polypodium trilobum*].

"To rid blood of impurities, such as collect in it during a serious illness, dry this plant [*püre*; not identified], then grind it to powder, and drink a decoction of it. This is a rare plant which grows in swamps; I know this because several times I helped a herbalist to

42

find it; we searched and searched and searched for it. After the impurities have been chased out of the blood, drink a decoction of this grass—we call it *kegni* [*Fascicularia bicolor*]."

He now held up his last two specimens: *külmai* blossoms (*quilmay; Elytropus chilensis Mull*) and yellow *fülel* flowers (*Solidago microglossa*). He looked at them somewhat tenderly and thoughtfully and then, in a confidential tone of voice and manner, said: "If a person becomes sick suddenly and acts as though he were sleeping, rouse him. Make him inhale the fumes of these two flowers. Make fumes quickly by putting the flowers into an olla or similar container and set it on glowing embers. If it is a child who acts that way, tell his mother to hold him in her arms, throw a cover over him and the fumes, and in this way force him to inhale them. These fumes will drive out the spirit of sickness that has gotten into that person or child. Someone has sent the evil spirit of sickness into him."

He then went on to tell that parts of the body affected with rheumatic pain should be rubbed down with an ointment made by mixing grease rendered from the fat of a fox, skunk, or puma with bile of sheep or cattle. The pain of burns can be relieved by applying the urine of the burned person. "Often," he added, "materials of a person's body have healing properties for that body, but for none other. Or, if you prefer, you can smear blood from the comb of a chicken on the burns. A nosebleed ends quickly if the bleeder snuffs powder of singed flamingo feathers. We have no flamingos in our country; we get these feathers from Argentina."

Huenun was certain that all curative knowledge originated in dreams: "One person who has such knowledge can tell another what he knows. I learned the use of one plant from a woman who is a specialist in its use. I want to tell you about her knowledge. I once had eczema, and I conferred with this woman because my relatives said that she had a cure—they urged me to go to her. I went to her even though I could have gone to a man herbalist whom I knew. The following night this woman learned in a dream of a herb that would cure my eczema. In the morning she searched for the herb

43

and found it; it was the *nülpi* [*Vicia valdiviana*]. She made an ointment from it and applied it to my eczema, which soon vanished. I have often wondered how she can dream a cure; maybe she thinks about it during the daytime and then dreams about it at night. Whatever it is these herbalists do, the interesting thing is that they always dream the right cure. There was a woman herbalist around here for years who dreamed every remedy she used, and she was more than one hundred years old when she died.

"I had a dream once that I related to an old man who said it was an important dream, for it had a cure. But I doubted then that it had a cure, and still do. I had the dream about twenty years ago when I was sick for four days and nights with a high temperature and could eat nothing. On the fourth day, after the sun had gone behind the Cordillera, I fell asleep. I dreamed that a beautiful old woman came to me with many boys and girls. She massaged me, and then each of the children did also. Just as the woman asked me for something to eat, I woke up. I was glad it was a dream, for I had nothing for her to eat—I was poorer then than I am now." He laughed about this.

He then spoke of the cause of sickness. "Until recently," he said, "we believed that all sickness was caused by the evil spirit of sickness, unless there was an obvious cause, such as a falling twig injuring an eye. People are now beginning to believe that there are other causes for sicknesses, and it is the *machis* who can discover the real causes by means of their powers. Chileans say *machis* are sorcerers and witches. It is true, a *machi* may be a sorcerer or sorceress, but if he is, we have another name for him—*kalku* [witch]. There are *kalkus*, however, who are not *machis*. I want nothing to do with *kalkus* of any kind. I am speaking here of a *machi* who can be trusted and who does good to people and not of a *kalku*. A *machi* has power to discover the real cause of a sickness.

"Here is a case: The year after I was married, I became so sick that I was hardly able to walk. I had severe pains in my heart. [He pointed at his abdomen. Informants on the coastal range who had told of sickness in the heart had also indicated the abdomen as

44

the seat of it.] We tried all remedies of which we had knowledge, but none gave me relief. Relatives and other *Mapuches* then told me that my sickness was undoubtedly due to harm inflicted on me by someone, that this could be the only cause of such a severe sickness. I believed them, for I had already decided that such must be the cause. My relatives fetched a *machi* who listened to what we said and agreed that someone had done me harm. He began to treat me. First, he pretended to stab me with a knife—he did not do so actually, of course—and then he sucked the point of sickness in my heart, the place in which I had severe pain, and out came a great deal of green-looking and vile-smelling matter. The next day I began to feel better. Before he treated me, I agreed to pay him a horse. Yes, I paid that *machi* the last horse I then owned, and I am still grateful to him for curing me."

He went on to tell more about the spirit of sickness. "Anyone," he continued, "can poke a hole into the skin of a sick person at the place in which he has pain and can suck blood from there, but it is only the *machi* who can suck out the spirit of sickness, the spirit that causes that sickness. Here is how it is generally done: On the spot that the person indicates as the source of pain, the *machi* puts a stone and twigs of either canelo, which we call *foique* [*Drimys winteri*], *chillko* [*fuscia*; *Fuchsia macrostemma*], or *paupauweñ* (esparto; *Luzuriaga radicans*). The stone must be one of those powerful ones; just any stone will not do. The *machi* knows which stone to use, and usually he owns one. He selects twigs of the proper plant, the one that will be most efficacious in the sickness he is treating, and he lets the twigs and stone rest on the area of pain for a short time before removing them. Then he bites the spot of pain and sucks it, bites it and sucks it, bites it and sucks it, until finally he spits out either a fly or a worm or a small lizard or maybe a figurine. Whatever he spits out generally does not show life, but on occasions its head or tail does move."

I ventured to ask Huenun if he believed that these objects were actually sucked out of the body. Francisca said in an undertone: "Your question is dynamite for his pride."

45

He showed resentment at being interrupted, but he answered: "Some say the *machi* sucks them out, but others say he has them in his mouth and merely spits them out. Whatever he does is beside the point right now. The *machi* now spits saliva and whatever he has sucked out on a canelo leaf and drops all into the fireplace. Immediately the sick person feels better. There are both men and women *machis* who treat by sucking, but not every *machi* does so. Some say certain *machis* have their finger tips split, and with them draw out the spirit of sickness. Our *machis* do not make incisions at the elbow or temple as you said some of your indigenous people do, but there is a *machi* in Quilche who makes a little cut with glass wherever the pain is and lets blood flow from that place. But I think he learned that from Chileans. I have never had an incision made in me, but I would, if I had pain and somebody advised that it be done."

He closed the door now, and in a quiet, confidential manner told us that persons become sick, at times, because someone poisons them. Poisoning is done with bile of snakes or frogs or with the juice of a plant called *pinaka* (cicuta mayor; *Conium maculatum*). Whatever is used, it is put into the food or drink of the victim. A person so poisoned gradually loses vitality and weight and eventually dies unless an antidote is used. Certain herbs are antidotes, and only a *machi* or a herbalist knows which ones. Huenun said that other causes of sickness are "the *anchimalléns*. The *anchimalléns* cannot be trusted; they bring sickness to families, even death."

"Who are they?" I asked.

"They? They are about so tall [indicating eighteen inches, approximately], and when they laugh, their teeth shine like lights. When I was still a young man, I once accompanied an older man to a *machitun* [performance over a sick person by a *machi*] at night-time. As we walked along, we came to an oak tree and saw lights on its trunk. Those were *anchimalléns*."

"Maybe it was gas that rose out of a marsh or maybe gas emitted by a rotten tree trunk," I ventured.

"No, indeed not," he replied. "A rotten tree trunk? Oh, no! It

46

was a healthy, very healthy tree trunk! And whatever you mean by gas coming out of a marsh, I am sure I do not know. I am telling you those lights were *anchimalléns*! I saw *anchimalléns* another time, too. One night, some years ago, my dogs kept on barking. I got up to see why. Maybe someone is in my wheat field, I thought. There they were, not far away, two *anchimalléns*, dancing: they came toward each other and backed away from each other. They repeated this several times and then disappeared. I went back into the *ruka*, hoping that no *kalku* had sent these two to our house to do us harm. Maybe they did do us harm; I do not know, but a few years later my daughter died."

It was time now for dinner. We had a dinner of roast pigeon, boiled potatoes, salad of garden lettuce, a soup thickened with fresh garden vegetables, and blackberries for dessert. Huenun ate of everything except the blackberries; he made some remark about blackberries not being friends of *Mapuches*. After dinner, he hobbled his horse in a different grazing place, lay down on the grass nearby, and took a siesta. Before long he returned.

"And now I want to tell you about the *machitun*," he began. "The *machitun* is a treatment given a very sick person. It is seldom performed until all other known remedies have been tried and have failed. A *machi* is the performer. We have always had both men and women *machis*, as I told you before, but today most of them are women. The family of the sick person chooses a *machi* and asks her to treat the sick person. She arrives just as darkness is setting in and begins her work and does not leave until day begins to break.

"I shall tell you of a *machitun* which I attended a year ago, and then of one that I attended last night. A year ago, the sick person was a relative of mine, and I was invited to be a yeller at the treatment. The *machi* ordered all of the sick man's clothes to be removed. Then he lay nude on the floor of his *ruka*. Then she put two twigs of canelo under his head—there is something sacred about the canelo tree, you know. Next she ordered the evil spirit of sickness to leave him, and after that placed small flat stones on his body, here and there and there and here, and on top of each, a red berry,

47

seeds of esparto. She then sat down between the sick person and the fireplace of the *ruka* and beat her *kultrugn*. [He explained that a *kultrugn* was made by hollowing out one end of a section of tree trunk and stretching a piece of hide over this end.] The *machi* sang her own songs, such songs as only she may sing; no one else would venture to sing them. In fact, I do not know the words of songs of any *machis*, and since I have become a Christian, I have paid little attention to the words used by them at any time. All I know is that the words of their songs are addressed to the spirit of good health. I know this *machi* was asking the spirit of health to drive the spirit of sickness from this sick person. [Francisca suspected that he knew the words, but did not wish to repeat them for fear of evil consequences. After all, the *machi* might also have powers to do harm.] All persons present stood behind the *machi*, including me. Just as she ended her song, we all yelled '*Ya-ah!*' The yell was directed to the spirit of good health.

"Now the *machi* began her investigation, that is, she looked for the cause of the sickness. She prepared herself by biting into canelo twigs to purify her tongue and teeth. Just as she did this, the red esparto berry that rested on that part of the body where the cause of the sickness was located raised itself. I saw this, and I have seen esparto berries do this at other *machituns*, also. Immediately the *machi* set to work to bite and suck this spot of my relative's body. Soon she spat out either a worm or a lizard—I do not know which, for I could not see well from where I stood. The thing that she spat out was the cause of the sickness—it was the evil spirit of this particular illness.

"Now, I want to be honest with myself and must tell you that I am positively certain that this part of the treatment, namely sucking out the worm or lizard, is faked. I noticed by your earlier question that you, too, suspected it was faked. I have never believed this to be anything but a hoax, but in spite of this hoax, seriously sick persons often recover after the performance of the *machitun*.

"The canelo twigs and other leaves or twigs that the *machi* had used, she now ordered thrown into the fireplace. Next she ordered

48

my relative to stand near the fire. That man was so weak that several men had to support him. While he was standing there, being supported, the *machi* swung a black hen toward him, walking completely around him four times while doing so. Each time she said, 'This man did nothing to you, you evil spirit of sickness. Leave him!' Since the spirit of evil is black, the hen also must be black. Sometimes the hen is killed after the swinging and the prayer, but more often she is chased out of the *ruka* onto the campo. She is not tolerated around where people are—she now has within her the spirit of the patient's sickness. My relative recovered.

"And now I want to tell you about the *machitun* that was performed between sundown and sunrise last night. I was again invited to be a yeller." The details varied somewhat from the one conducted over his relative. Near the sick person's head the *machi* placed two canelo twigs vertically into the ground and hung a small kettle between them. Into the kettle she put canelo tips, flowers of fuchsias, and esparto berries, and then she sat to the left of the sick person, beat her *kultrugn*, and sang one of her songs. All yellers yelled in high-pitched, prolonged tones, but ended by yelling "*Ya-ah!*" several times in varying tones. Next the *machi* vigorously shook a dried gourd containing pebbles and sang two more songs. Each song was concluded by yellers yelling as before. The *machi* now smoked a pipe and blew smoke upon the sick person, and then in pleading tones she begged the spirit of sickness to leave the body of the sick person.

"How does the spirit of sickness get into a body?" I asked.

"That is easily answered," he replied. "The spirit of sickness can be sent into the water that we drink and the food that we eat. I told you before that it is through these ways that they enter the body."

Another variation was a fourth song with the yellers' response. A liaison now talked to the *machi*—the sick person was too ill to do so himself. It was a prolonged pleading that the *machi* cure the sick person, and the *machi* was repeatedly told that only she had the knowledge and power to do so. Following the pleading, the *machi*

49

set to work to produce a cure: She called on her powers and then gave an order for someone to snip the ear of a sheep and bring her a few drops of its blood in a cup. While the blood was being taken, she sang another song of petition—this time to the rhythm of a rattle made from a dried gourd containing esparto seeds, not pebbles. She next took canelo tips from the kettle and rubbed them between the palms of her hands until her palms were well covered with sap. Then she mixed the sap with the sheep's blood and smeared this mixture over the entire body of the sick person. Next she placed a few canelo leaves and several pebbles—she took the pebbles from the rattle she had used earlier—on the aching part of the sick man's body.

After this she danced to the right of him—the pain was localized on that side. (Huenun imitated the dance: he took a few staccato hops forward, walked a few steps, took another set of staccato hops forward.) The *machi* danced in this manner four times, from the man's head to his feet. After each of the first three dances, she walked briskly back toward the man's head; but during the fourth dance, she stopped abruptly in line with the place where the man's pain was. She brushed the canelo leaves and stones off, chewed the leaves, and then rubbed her teeth and tongue with them. And now came the tense moment: She leaned over the sick man and sucked from the aching place the cause of the sickness. She showed the bystanders what she had sucked out. (Huenun could not come close enough to see it.) She looked at everyone present and said to all, "If it is the will of *Chau*, the spirit of sickness will leave this man, and he will recover." She sang a last song, one that let everyone know she had completed the *machitun* and was leaving. All yellers yelled a final "*Ya-ah!*" and all was finished.

"Most *machis* want to be paid in advance," Huenun added. "The amount depends on the family's ability to pay and on the type of sickness to be treated. I know one *machi* who always asked for a horse, or a similar large animal, and fifty to one hundred pesos in addition. Now I have told you all that I know about the *machitun*, and I must go home."

50

We paid Huenun this day with a sack of wheat. "Flour is good, too," he said, "but my wife likes to grind wheat on her metate; she can then make *Mapuche* dishes from it, something she cannot do with flour from the mill. She will be glad to have this wheat." We shook hands, and Huenun was gone.

CHAPTER VI

Witches and Magic

Margaret and I decided, while transcribing the notes on the *machitun*, that we needed additional information on *machis* and their activities. We jotted down questions that we would ask Huenun: How did the *machi* become a *machi*? What did Huenun mean by *machis'* powers? What was the origin of these powers? What is there that is sacred about the canelo tree? Did he ever bite on canelo twigs to purify his teeth? What happened to the hen eventually? How many yellers were there at a *machitun*? What would happen if a person invited to yell absented himself? And there were more questions. I decided that we should begin with the one about the hen. If Huenun should resent being asked for further information on *machis* and *machituns*, we would ask him about death, an item about which we had only slight information.

However, there was this problem: In what mood will Huenun be when he comes again? Will he want to lead the interview? Will he resent being asked for more information on a topic which we have already discussed with him? Francisca warned us. On the coastal range we had learned that asking such questions was considered a reflection on the informant's ability to tell a thing well the first time. There, informants vehemently resisted such questioning. We did not want to offend Huenun, but I decided I would try, and see what the outcome would be. I knew Huenun could answer our questions, since he had been a participant in *machituns*. After all, I said, Panguipulli is not on the coastal range; people in Panguipulli valley may be different. Margaret added, "They speak a dialect of the Araucanian language different from that spoken on the coastal range. Maybe they are different in other ways, too." Our decision made, we blew out our kerosene lamp and went to bed.

When morning came, we attended Mass with the mission sisters. Margaret replenished the fire in our little potbellied stove—Francisca, always thoughtful, had started the fire early—and we ate a nourishing breakfast. We took a short brisk walk along a verdant ravine filled with brush and undergrowth—the kind in which a puma might well have lurked. We returned by a path through a wheat field and viewed again the Andean ranges and silently and with awe admired their snow-capped volcanoes.

Exhilarated by the morning mountain air, we returned to the classroom and prepared for work. Margaret set chairs in their accustomed places: hers at one end of the table, mine to her right at the side of the table, the one for Francisca to my right, and Huenun's opposite mine.

Not long after, Huenun arrived. He complained that he had lost sleep during the night because of the ferocious barking of his dogs. Worry that a puma had gotten into his sheepfold kept him from sleeping soundly, even after the dogs quit barking; however, he found all the sheep alive and well in the morning—something for which he was grateful.

"Huenun," I began very casually, "Margaret and I wondered if you would tell us a little more about the *machi* and her powers. We were wondering last evening when rewriting that worthwhile information you gave us about the *machitun* just what happened to the hen that was chased away from the *machitun*, the one possessed with the spirit of sickness?"

Pointing at Margaret, but his eyes flashing at me in an unfriendly way, "Has that girl any intelligence?" he spurted.

I answered him in his tone of voice and tried to put resentment into my eyes, too, "That girl? Indeed she has! One reason why I brought her to Chile and to the *Mapuches* all the way from North America was because of her great and keen intelligence!"

53

"In that case," he retorted, "she has the answer in her notebook. I saw her put it there yesterday! If it is not there, she lacks intelligence and there is no use telling it again! Let us go on to something else." And on to something else we went!

"Tell me, Huenun," I began in a meek voice, but boiling inside, "does a *Mapuche* ever have a premonition of death?"

"Yes," he answered just as meekly, "I know several ways. For example, if a *choñchoñ* circles around a *ruka* at night, giving out calls and weird cries, a person in that *ruka* will soon die. Near my *ruka* there is a row of trees, and one time a *choñchoñ* called and cried out there. I knew at once that one of us would die, for that *choñchoñ* flew in and out of that row of trees, then back and forth, and then straight along the entire row. Not long after that one of my daughters took sick and died. *Choñchoñ*, they say, comes from the south. He is never seen but only heard; in fact, he is invisible. If he cries in one place and you go there, he is already crying in another place; if you go there, he will have flown to still another place. [On the coastal range we had heard *choñchoñ* stories, also. Non-Araucanians there said *choñchoñ* was undoubtedly a night bird; Francisca was of the same opinion.]

"When my daughter took sick that time, she vomited for days and could not eat. I did not want to believe that she would die, but since we had been told that a Turk near here was saying that he could foretell death, I went to him and said, 'I have a sick girl. I want to know if she will live or die.' 'Pay me five pesos,' said the Turk. I did so, and then he wrote on a piece of paper: 'Your girl is very sick. I do not know if she will recover. I can better foretell if I go to your place to see her and study her sickness. If you want me to do this, you will have to pay me with a sheep, and that in advance.' I brought him the sheep, and he came to my *ruka* and studied the sickness. 'Maybe,' he said, 'I can cure the girl, but before I attempt it, you must pay me one hundred pesos.' Since I did not have that much money, he was satisfied with a two-year-old cow. The next day my daughter died. I went to him and told him that she had died and that he ought to compensate me with fifty or one hundred pesos. He answered that he had done what he had promised to do and that he would not pay me one centavo. That man must be in hell! At least that is where he belongs!

"Occasionally," he went on to say, "a man has a dream that foretells his death. A relative of mine repeatedly dreamed that he would die, and he was afraid to die. To prevent his death, he conducted a *gnillatun* [the tribal religious ceremonial]. I myself have had dreams that I think are significant, but I have never dreamed that I would die. I had a dream some years ago about a bird called *klegnklegn*—Chileans call this bird a falcon—this is the bird that looks as though it had a white cloth tied about its neck with the ends hanging down over its breast. Well, in my dream this bird was flying high when suddenly it swooped down with great noise and sat on my right shoulder. [He told this with much pantomiming.] Just as this happened, I woke up. The blood of the *klegnklegn* has within itself great power. My grandfather once killed one, sucked some of its blood, and injected it into a vein in his right hand. Doing this gave that hand extra strength. On one occasion when one of his wives argued with him, he hit her with that hand and killed her. I had another dream about a bird. Three or four years ago, or maybe seven or eight, after my *klegnklegn* dream, I dreamed that I was on horseback on top of a hill in Kenchuri. A beautiful bird, a tame one, a very shiny one, came and sat on my left forearm; it was so tame that I could stroke it. Then I woke up. Well, these two dreams have increased my intelligence and my understanding of things and have given me direction as to what I should do, but neither seems to have foretold my death.

"I had a dream not long ago that may be significant—I cannot tell. I was in a large meadow of rolling land, land like that out there [he pointed out the window]. There was a white altar there, and my wife and I were laid near it, wrapped in bedding. Candles burned all about us. I do not know what this dream means.

"I had another dream. A poor *huinca* and I were on an arid rock, and a sister came along driving a noisy, two-wheeled coach drawn by two white horses. The cover of the coach was transparent; we could see bread inside. Suddenly the coach stopped, and the sister gave us bread. We ate the bread and drank water from a hole in the arid rock." He remarked, then, that he did not wish to live much longer and that he did not want to be an old man. I asked him if he had any idea how much longer he would live. He answered, "No one knows that."

"The *Mapuche* who was buried yesterday had no premonition of his death," he went on to say. "Many other persons, however, knew that he would not live to be old; he had too many enemies, persons from whom he had stolen when he was young. There was no doubt that sooner or later one of them would send an evil spirit of sickness into that man, and this is probably what happened. If it was not one of his enemies who did so, it must have been done by the old woman he had taken as wife, one who has always been spoken of as being a *kalku*. After she was with him only three or four months, he sent her away. It is significant that this one was not at his funeral yesterday; his other wife was."

"Did they perform the *machitun* over this man?" I asked.

"No, not this man; he did not believe in the powers of the *machitun*; he was always a good Christian," Huenun answered.

Margaret, as she set out to replenish the fire, said to herself in an undertone, "Always a good Christian? I wonder about that!"

On the coastal range a person who is dying is dressed in his best clothes, but without shoes and hat. Relatives and other persons present dress him. Huenun agreed that this was an Araucanian custom. "Why should he wear a hat and shoes now, when he never did so in life? It has never been our custom to wear shoes or hats," he remarked, "except when we go where there are Chileans or other *huincas*." He went on to tell that a band woven of yarn is brought around the dying man's forehead and tied in a knot at the back. Formerly all men wore similar headbands to keep their hair out of their eyes. A dying woman, too, is dressed as women generally dress. Formerly, a man's personal silver ornaments were buried with him, and so were a woman's buried with her.

"About twenty years ago," Huenun continued, "men began to

rob graves of these ornaments. Two men did so in our cemetery here. We saw them do it and chided them. We reported them to Chilean police, but nothing was done about it. If one knew where to search for silver ornaments, one could find them buried in pottery. I know of a sterile wife of a former cacique who buried her silver ornaments in that way. It is a custom with us that a mother give her silver things to one of her daughters, but this woman had no daughters, and she did not want any other woman to have her ornaments. Several times I have plowed up pottery, but none had silver ornaments in it. This pottery has a different color from ours; it must have belonged to a people who lived here before we did. We call such pottery *traiki*; ours that is buried we call *wishugn*."

I then told him of a mourning custom of some North American Indians whereby a woman, at the death of a loved one, severs a joint of a finger as a sign of great sorrow. To this he replied: "My grandfather told me many of our old customs, but he never told me of such a one. That makes no sense. We had a custom formerly, according to my uncle, whereby a husband, if he was a rich man, was expected to give a cow or a horse to the parents of his recently deceased wife. If he was a poor man, he gave silver ornaments, like silver spurs, and if he had maltreated his wife at any time, he was obliged to give more. But this is no longer done. Today, some of our women do as Chilean women do around here: When their fathers or mothers or husbands or children die, they let their hair hang unbraided, only tied back. This is done for one year. Our women in mourning have never worn their silver ornaments while mourning, and they do not wear them today, not even at fiestas."

At this point some children came to tell Huenun that the saddle had fallen off his horse—he had hobbled the horse, as usual, on a nearby grassy plot. He went out, replaced the saddle, talked to the horse a while, and returned. With some humor he remarked, "Maybe I should not tell you any more of our old customs; spirits must have thrown the saddle off my horse to show their displeasure—the saddle was thrown over the horse's head! This never happens under normal conditions; saddles should fall to one side of the horse. I have a good friend who was plowing with a pair of oxen one time, and every time he stopped to talk to a passer-by or to look around a little, the yoke was thrown off those oxen. There is a spirit world, you know, that does these things to show approval or disapproval of what we do. I am pretty certain that the spirits threw that saddle off my horse.

"There are bad spirits in some of our lakes. I know a *machi* who can act through them," he went on to say. "In Lake Calefquén there is a spirit called Caleochu. Caleochu pulled a boat into the lake recently and drowned the seven persons in it. I once saw lights in that lake. Volcano Shoshuenco has a bad spirit, too. Shoshuenco has only one araucaria tree [*pewen* or *pehuén*; *Araucaria araucana*], which is on its sunset side and, therefore, has wonderfully long and meaty nuts. [He indicated these to be four times the length from tip of thumb to first knuckle.] But if anyone should climb the sides of Shoshuenco to get those nuts, he would turn into a snake. The winds that blow across Shoshuenco bring bad insects with them. Shoshuenco has a bad spirit, I can assure you.

"The first eruption of volcanoes that I remember was when Shoshuenco attacked Volcano Villarrica. I do not know exactly when it happened, but I remember we were already living in a *ruka* made of boards. We had moved because my wife no longer wanted to live where we were because we had no view. We had a fine orchard though, but we have a fine one now, too. Very well! The first activities we saw of that eruption were like lightning. Lightning came from both Shoshuenco and Villarrica, and then balls of fire of this size [gesturing to indicate one foot in diameter] appeared. They were being hurled by Shoshuenco at Villarrica, and Villarrica retaliated. In this way they carried on for some time, hurling brimstones at each other with great swiftness. Shoshuenco finally blew out his top, but in doing so, he died."

I remarked, "This must have been a frightening thing. I would have been filled with fear!"

"Fear?" said Huenun. "No, I had no fear in me, but I did say a prayer to *Chau*. A herbalist was with us at the time, and she

58

noticed that I had no fear and remarked about it. This herbalist was a *machi*, but she never performed a *machitun*." I wondered if Huenun had any scientific knowledge regarding volcanic eruptions and asked him if he had ever heard anyone give an explanation of why volcanoes erupt.

Promptly he answered, "I just told you that it is a bad spirit in the volcano that does so! Shoshuenco has one of these bad spirits. Shoshuenco, today, is still possessed with that bad spirit.

"Villarrica, on the contrary," he went on to say, "gives the impression of having a good spirit, but I sometimes wonder if he can be trusted. He does show a good spirit when he lets people have the nuts that grow on his araucaria trees; he wants to nourish people with them. But not too long ago he erupted by himself, and we were really afraid that he would blow himself to pieces. He was angry at the time with one of those Chilean *fundo* owners, and for three days he blew out many, many, many red-hot stones. These melted the snow on all of his sides and caused creeks to swell into rivers and rivers into uncontrollable torrents. Whole areas were flooded. Since this eruption was forecast, and since people knew that it would happen, they should have conducted a *gnillatun* to prevent it.

"Here is what had happened: An old man—he was an old-timer for he still wore a chiripa—was taking the liberty of walking across a Chilean's *fundo*, a *fundo* located at the foot of Villarrica. This *fundo* owner was known to be rich. He not only owned much land, but on it he had a sawmill. He also owned a threshing machine. The old man came to the owner's house and asked him for a drink of water, but the owner refused to give it to him. Next, the old man asked for bread, and again the owner refused him. Then the old man gave him a warning. 'For your unkindness to me and for cutting down araucaria trees on Villarrica, you can expect something to happen to you,' he said, and then walked up Villarrica in great haste. The owner sent one of his *inquilinos* to see where the old man had gone, but he could find him nowhere. His footsteps, however, could be seen on the side of Villarrica—those footsteps were far apart, in fact, two to three meters apart. In due time Villarrica erupted. Water came gushing down his sides, as I told you, and swept away not only the topsoil of a good portion of that Chilean's *fundo* but also his sawmill and his threshing machine. That old man was the spirit of Villarrica."

"Did any *Mapuches* lose their lives?" I asked.

"Very few; most of them got away," he replied. "Some lost their *rukas*. One young man told me that the howling of Villarrica and the noise made by stones rolling down his sides was terrific. Since neither he nor his parents could sleep, they walked to a higher elevation about two hundred meters from where they were. While there they saw their *ruka* taken away by an avalanche of snow and rock. Some *Mapuches* who had *rukas* near the shores of Lake Villarrica had to flee because of the sizzling steam caused by glowing lava flowing into the lake, and others had to leave because the lake overflowed its banks—much water flowed into the lakes from streams of melted snows. When lands are flooded, we say it is like the days of *tripako*—*tripako* is the word our old people use when they tell a story of a flood. That story you can read in your own Bible, too; Father Sigifredo calls it the Story of the Deluge.

"This is the story of the days of *tripako* as told by our old people: It happened very, very, very long ago. When *tripako* was on, many people died in other places, but no one died where the *Mapuches* lived, and for this reason: There is a mountain called Lanco Huellahue. On it a good spirit formed a hill, which is called *tregntregn*. As the waters of the flood rose, people took refuge on *tregntregn*. There they sacrificed a girl, one about ten years old, one so young still that she had not yet known evil. They removed her heart and threw her body into the water—the water had begun to rise all around them. Everyone now prayed to *Chau*. When the prayer was finished, the girl's heart, too, was thrown into the water.—This is different from the *gnillatun*. There the heart of a sheep is consumed by fire while those who are leading the *gnillatun* look on.—As soon as the girl was sacrificed, *tregntregn* started to grow two pillars, one of gold and one of silver. The people climbed

60

on top of these pillars to save themselves. As the water rose, the pillars grew taller; hence, the people were always safe on them. That is the story of *tripako*. Today, we use the word *tripako* when we say Lake Villarrica is rising because Volcano Villarrica is erupting."

Relating this story reminded him of another told about a flood. "When I was a little boy," he began, "an old man told me that one time a bull stopped the regular flow of a river by standing crosswise in it. As the water rose, it overflowed its banks and flooded all the area. About this time a man and a woman came along, carrying a lance. With it they stabbed the bull, and his blood colored the water red. That is all there is to that story. Father Sigifredo says the story makes him think of the Passage through the Red Sea."

After we had refreshments, I asked Huenun if the *Mapuches* ever prayed to spirits, such as the spirit of Villarrica. "No, not to those spirits," he answered. "We pray to *Chau*; we have always prayed to *Chau*. Spirits occupy stones, too, we know, but we do not pray to them. We pray only to *Chau*.

"In Argentina there are small stones, both round ones and flat ones, which have short legs with little feet and can move about. Each has a spirit within itself, a spirit that can convert itself into a cat or a dog or some other animal or into a *huinca* or a Gaucho. A relative of mine brought one of these stones back with him from Argentina. He had seen this one walk while he was herding sheep on an *estancia* there, picked it up, brought it home, and put it into his corral with his animals. Now, we here, on this side of the Cordillera, have a custom that when a large animal is killed, a snip of its ear is taken and thrown into the fire—this is a sacrifice to *Chau*. But in Argentina this snip is cut into small pieces and with some of the blood of the animal is given to such a stone by the owner of it. If this offering is neglected, the spirit of the stone is liable to harm the man's animals; it may even send sickness into them and kill them all. My relative never neglected to make the sacrifice to the stone. Such a stone is called *wichalkura* when used by ordinary people; when used by a *machi*, it is called *lican*."

61

I should like to have asked at this point how the animals in his relative's corral fared and in whose possession the stone was now. But it was best not to interrupt. He went right on to tell of another stone that possessed magic. "There is a stone we call *llanka*, which is by far the most powerful stone. This stone has a hole in its center; the *lican* does not. Our old people have always said that the *llanka* belonged to a people who lived here before the *Mapuches*. I know a *Mapuche*—he lives according to our old way, like all *Mapuches* lived formerly—who got himself a *llanka* from a *kalku* who lives on the Pacific Coast. Every year when cattle are branded and sheep's ears are snipped to show ownership [following an order issued by the Chilean Government], this man takes the blood of his cattle and the snips from the ears of his sheep and puts them into a piece of pottery along with his *llanka*. He then wraps the pottery in a poncho and buries all in his corral. I have seen him do this. There is an old *Mapuche* belief that a *llanka* then turns into a bird or into a large animal and goes out among the owner's horses and cows and sheep and helps them multiply."

He sat thoughtfully for a moment and then said, "But a man who has too many animals had better curtail their increase lest he become so wealthy that some persons will become jealous of him and hire a *kalku* to do him harm." Then Huenun added with emphasis, "Those *kalkus* are despicable persons! One *kalku* learns her black art from another, usually an older one. We have had three powerful *kalkus* in this valley. I have known all three. The one still living is related to me. I detest *kalkus*! They are contemptible persons! Insincere!"

One of Huenun's neighbors told him that he had seen the one related to Huenun busy herself near the roots of an old tree that stood in his fields. After she left, the neighbor dug around the roots of the tree and found a chicken gizzard there in a little hole. He took the gizzard to another *kalku*, one who had antidotes for witchcraft. This *kalku* examined the gizzard, threw it into a river nearby, and said nothing. Huenun reasoned that the *kalku* must have used an

62

antidote, for how else could it have been that nothing happened to that man's field?

Huenun was certain that witchcraft had been used on his own fields. "This was three years ago," he began. "I had a scanty harvest then and have had an insufficient one ever since. Last year while I was grubbing blackberry bushes in one of my fields, I noticed the tail feathers of chickens showing above the ground nearby. I pulled them out, dug deeper, and found a chicken gizzard there. This fall my harvest is so poor that I shall have to buy seeds when planting time comes again. I am harvesting only enough wheat to satisfy my family's needs between now and planting time.

"I am convinced it is the *kalku* who still lives in this area who is doing damage to my fields," he went on. "Her family is angry with me. They say that the land which I cultivate belongs to them. But this is not true. My wife was given that land by her father; in fact, we should lay claim to more land than this, for her father wanted us to have an additional piece of land. Her father wrote on a sheet of paper, while he was still living, a description of the land and the exact section of it that he had in mind. The sad thing is that we cannot find out who has this paper; someone must have it. If we could only find out who has it, we would know which additional piece of land it is that we should claim. Maybe this *kalku* has the paper. My wife and the *kalku's* husband had the same father, but my wife is the daughter of her father's first wife, and the *kalku's* husband is a son of his second wife. Now, the father gave more land to the children of his first wife than to those of his second wife— that is known by everyone—and that is why the *kalku* and her group are jealous of us. My wife's father also recorded his land with the cacique—all land was so recorded then—but that was thirty years ago, at a time when each cacique still recorded all lands owned by the *Mapuches* under him. I would like to have recourse to these records, but I am told that they are no longer available. When I found that gizzard, I should have hired a *kalku* to undo the harm being done to my fields, but I detest dealing with *kalkus* because they are despicable persons." Francisca suggested that he try spreading fertilizer on his field. "A sack of it costs more pesos than I can get together in a year," Huenun replied.

"Why not collect the cow dung from the pasture lands and use it as fertilizer," suggested Francisca. He gave her a disdainful look and said nothing.

I asked him why he did not take his problem to the Chilean Court of Claims and Grievances for Araucanians. He replied that he would do so if the court were still in Valdivia—the judges there had always given Araucanians a fair hearing and an honest deal— but this is not true of the present court.

He then told of an instance of revenge in which witchcraft was inflicted on an entire family: "A whole pack of *kalkus* was hired. They met in secret session—we call this *reniruka*—and sent sickness upon this family, a sickness called *moilfun kutran*. This sickness is a fearful thing; blood comes from the mouth and the nose. When a *Mapuche* does this to a Chilean—or if he only bewitches the Chilean's fields—the Chilean retaliates by using a sorcerer to bring blindness on the culprit. You may be certain of one thing: wherever evil is done, a *kalku* is involved."

We had heard on the coastal range that when bewitched meat was found in fields—it had been buried there—it was hung over the fireplace in the *ruka*. As the meat shrank, the culprit's body, too, shrank, and eventually he died unless the offended person took pity on him and removed the meat. Huenun had not heard of this, but he had seen a bewitched egg taken from a field and hung over the fireplace after two long needles had been stuck crisscross through it. It was hoped, he said, that because of this the one who had planted the egg in the field would become blind or lame or would die. He had also heard it said that persons who found bewitched meat in a field laid wood on the field in the form of a cross and built a fire in the four angles of it: it was believed that when this was done, no harm would come to the fields. "The great problem," Huenun said, with puzzled emphasis, "is to find the meat or the eggs. By the time one has good reason to suspect witchcraft,

64

the destruction of grain has already advanced too far to be ended by counter treatment.

"I want to tell you about one more of our beliefs, and then I must go home: It is of the help that good spirits of the world give us. Achicheo was a lion, a spirit who understood man, and in time of war he communicated with our people who were in various places. It must have been done as it is today; today, a man working out here on a hill by means of light communicates with someone in Santiago. Achicheo, also, had offices; these were within the earth. Pillikuchi occupied one of them; in fact, he lived in it. In Quilche, Achicheo had another office occupied by Kalfumallen, a spirit who accompanies man. When Pedro de Valdivia tried to exterminate the *Mapuches*, Achicheo and his helpers went with the *Mapuches* and assisted them in their fighting. Achicheo had a lasso made of fox hair—it looked like a snake—and with it he made bridges across rivers for *Mapuches* to use. The enemy in pursuit of the *Mapuches* would use the bridges also, but once they were halfway across, the bridges would collapse, fall into the river, and the enemy would completely disappear.

"Then there was another kind of bridge also used in time of war. This bridge built itself by its own power in places where a bridge was needed either to defeat the enemy or to flee from them.

"In the days of wars some *machis* had connections with spirits that came out of Volcano Villarrica. One such *machi* set up in a row stakes so high [indicated three to four feet] and prayed. Soon life came into the stakes, and they helped the *Mapuches* burn down the town of Villarrica.

"And now I have told you some more of our old *Mapuche* ways, some of which are still our customs. It is a pity that we still have those detestable *kalkus*. I must leave for home now."

I gave Huenun some money with which to buy wheat, the equivalent of a day's labor. He bade us *adiós* and rode off.

CHAPTER VII

Religious Beliefs and Ceremonials

Huenun seemed sad this morning. He explained that he could not help thinking of a relative who was buried the other day. "He died too soon," he lamented. "He was only sixty years old, or maybe seventy. He was my uncle on my father's mother's side and also an uncle of my wife. His grandfather was the first assistant to the great Cacique Katrinir, who belonged to one of the respected early day families of this area. We buried him in a coffin, as Chileans do. Until recently we buried everybody in a *trolof*, that is, in a tree trunk cut in halves lengthwise. Each half is dug out to look like a boat, and the body is placed between the halves. There is still, today, an occasional burial in a *trolof*.

"On my way home from the burial, I thought of our old religious beliefs and of our old way of speaking to *Chau*. I said to myself, 'Where is my relative now? Has he gone to the heaven of the *huincas*? Has he gone to *pillañ* where our people go when they die? Where is he now?' He told me once that he had a dream: Men were riding on horseback along the rim of a crater; they also danced there. They had a *trutruka* and carried banners." (Huenun had made a *trutruka* by splitting a *colihüe* stalk [*Chusquea culeou*] in halves, removing the core of each half, tying the halves into position again with blades of *chupón*, and then pulling an intestine of horse over it to hold all firmly together. The lower end of the *colihüe* he tipped off with a section of cow horn.) Huenun noted that his uncle had had the dream twice, each time just before sunrise—the first time about twenty years ago. Such a dream reveals that a soul will be well received in *pillañ*. Huenun sat there, sad and thoughtful.

I asked, "Where is *pillañ*, Huenun?"

"I do not know where your heaven is," he replied, "but *pillañ* is over there, near the volcanoes, near Villarrica, Shoshuenco, Quetropillán, and all the others. The *gnenpins* are in *pillañ*; everyone is there. We ask the *gnenpins* in *pillañ* to ask *Chau* to grant us what we need most at the time, just as you ask your saints for what you need—St. Isidore, St. Sebastian, and others.

"The *gnenpins* were prophets, when they were alive, who prophesied through their dreams. Such a man in Panguipulli was my grandfather. Generally, a *gnenpin* is a descendant of a cacique, but my grandfather was not one of these. *Gnenpins* play an important role among us. They are not only leaders in the *gnillatun*, but their judgments are significant and are greatly respected by caciques. In fact, it is sometimes the *gnenpin's* decisions that are followed in important matters rather than those of the cacique. In Quilche there was a highly respected *gnenpin* when I was a young man. There is only one *gnenpin* in this area today, an old woman whom everyone calls simply *Gnenpin*."

"How many prophets are there in *pillañ*?" I asked.

"I have no idea," he answered. "They are all there. How can anyone know their number! Why is it significant to know this? In *pillañ* are also old women whom we call *pillañ kuche*—at one time they beat drums for dances at the *gnillatun*. Do not ask me how many of these there are in *pillañ*; I do not know the answer."

I wished to know then whether God was in *pillañ*. "No, *Chau* is not in *pillañ*. He must be somewhere else," he answered. "Do you know where He is? We have three names for God: *Chau*, *Gnünechén*, and *Nünémapún*. We and you and all the *huincas* pray to the same God. I did not have to change my belief in God when I became a Christian; our God is the same as yours, only we call Him *Chau*—we have always called Him *Chau*. When we say Christian prayers today and the word God occurs in them, we say *Chau* instead of God. When we think and speak of *Chau* as ruling the world, we think and speak of Him as *Gnünechén*; when we speak of Him as having created the world and us, we call Him *Nünémapún*. My grandmother and uncles—not my grandfather, for he seldom told me anything—used to advise me to ask *Nünémapún*, the Creator of all things, to keep sickness away from my house and to protect my family. My grandparents, who lived before missionaries came here, were not Christians, but they knew that there was Somebody who had created them. When we think of the woman who is with *Chau*, we think of her as *wenümapu ñuke*, our mother, and we ask her to get for us from *Chau* what we are praying for." Francisca remarked that she had often wondered if this belief had its origin in the Catholic devotion to the Mother of Jesus. He replied: "No, no, *wenümapu ñuke* is not the mother of *Chau*; she is His wife, or woman. But nothing is ever said about children of these two.

"We offer two kinds of sacrifices—these are old customs. Persons offer small sacrifices at home, and families offer greater ones at the *gnillatun*. Small sacrifices are offered when lightning flashes and thunder blasts and rolls angrily around. On these occasions we put embers outside the *ruka* and drop kernels of wheat on them. Words are not needed; it is understood that the burning kernels are a prayer asking *tralkan* [spirit of thunder] not to hurt our place.

"Offerings of food are also made at home. When my grandmother cooked chicken and the boiling point was reached, she took a spoonful of broth, walked out of the *ruka* into the yard, and threw it heavenward with a prayer to *Chau* that our family would be blessed with more of everything, that all would go well with us, and that the spirit of sickness would not affect us. Also, before she handed food to anyone at mealtime, she threw a teaspoonful of it into the fire. She obliged no one else to make these offerings—there was no obligation even for her to do so. I have never made such offerings, but I saw her do it. All these were looked upon as small personal offerings.

"If the people wanted to pray together and offer sacrifice jointly, they conducted a *gnillatun*. But before I tell you about our *gnillatun*, I want to tell you about our caciques. It is the cacique

68

who gives orders that a *gnillatun* be conducted, and today, in our valley, practically the only right left to the cacique is to announce the holding of a *gnillatun* and then to direct it. Our cacique seldom conducts one now—other men do so. I hope that I can conduct one before too long."

Huenun now stressed the importance of caciques. "There have always been caciques," he said, "and always they were, and today are, the leaders of the people. Every *Mapuche* born has a right to the leadership of a cacique, and every *Mapuche* born in an area has a right, too, to possess land in it. It is the very fact that a man owns land in an area that puts him under the leadership of the cacique in that area. Every cacique knows the boundaries of the area over which he has jurisdiction, and because of the boundaries he knows who his people are. He knows who owns what pieces of land, for he has a record of the ownership of all land in the area—or at least he ought to have a record; it is one of his duties.

"A chief duty of the cacique is to call his people together and confer with them regarding the days on which a *gnillatun* is to be held, as I have already told you. If one is to be held jointly with families of other caciques, it is the duty of each cacique to send out an order to all families under him that they are to meet in *aillarewe*, a general assembly, with families of the other caciques. At the *aillarewe* the time for a joint *gnillatun* is agreed upon, and if there are other important matters pertaining to all families assembled, these, too, are discussed." He added that, when he was young, his family belonged to the *aillarewe* which met in Quilche. To Quilche came the caciques and the families of Mailef, Cudive, Coigue, and Malalhue. The great *gnenpin* lived in Quilche, and the most learned and authoritative cacique lived in Coigue. At present Huenun belongs to the *aillarewe* which meets in the Panguipulli area. To it come the people from Panguipulli, Colcod, and Tralcapulli. The most prominent and authoritative cacique in this group lives in Panguipulli.

"A man is a cacique," Huenun continued, "because his father before him was one, his father's father before that, and so back into time of long ago." A cacique has no insignia to indicate that he is a cacique, but everyone knows who the cacique is and speaks of him by his name. Formerly, if he was a wealthy man—many caciques were—he, like other wealthy men, wore a silver neckpiece with a breastplate dangling from it to let people know that he was a rich man. Huenun thought such ostentation unwise. Such a man, he said, was taking a chance of arousing jealousy and, consequently, of having his land bewitched.

Caciques in the past, Huenun went on to say, were the people's most prominent men, some more so than others. Katrinir was the best known of four caciques in the Panguipulli area. Other outstanding caciques of the past were Katrilaf, Allapan, Puelpan, Licanpan, and Katripan. Katripan's judgments were so highly respected that caciques from distances as far as Petrufquen came to confer with him. Also, if it happened that two caciques in what is now Argentina had a quarrel, someone from there came to fetch Katripan to settle the dispute. There was also Shaihueco, who lived on Lake Huechulafquen, on what is now the border between Argentina and Chile. His judgments, too, were sought in settling disputes on the Argentine side. I asked whether Araucanians who lived in what is now Chile and those who lived in what is now Argentina had ever warred on each other. He replied, "No, never! We have always been friends.

"And now I want to tell you about the *gnillatun*," continued Huenun. "As I told you, if the people want to pray together and to offer sacrifices jointly, they conduct a *gnillatun*. As I have already said, the decision to conduct one is made either by a cacique in conjunction with the fathers of families under him or by the caciques of several adjoining areas, if there is to be a joint ceremony. Formerly, on occasion, more than one thousand persons attended a joint *gnillatun*. The primary purpose of the *gnillatun* is to ask *Chau* for favorable weather at harvest time. Since it is now harvest time, many *Mapuches* talk about conducting a *gnillatun* because unfavorable weather would be a disaster. At all other times, a *gnillatun* is held only when a calamity threatens the people or an individual.

70

When I was a very small boy, Volcano Llanquihue erupted: he threw ashes as far as Panguipulli and everything was white with them. Everybody hurriedly prepared for a *gnillatun* in answer to the call of the cacique, and small sacrifices were being offered at home while preparations were being made for the large one. I remember, also, an earthquake, a very severe and alarming one. Everyone hurriedly made preparations then, too, for a *gnillatun*. Today, we also conduct a *gnillatun* immediately after a destructive windstorm subsides or while an unending rain is destroying our grain or when an epidemic breaks out among our animals or among the people."

Huenun then told of the origin of the *gnillatun*. "Our old people have always taught that the *Mapuches* have conducted *gnillatuns* uninterruptedly since *tregntregn* was formed, and have never neglected to perform them. This is how the *gnillatun* originated: Shortly after *tregntregn* appeared, a *gnenpin*—he lived about two kilometers from present Panguipulli—had a dream in which he was told that our people should offer animals as sacrifices to *Chau*. Since then we have never failed to do so. Sacrificial offerings of animals are the important ceremonial of the *gnillatun*. In his dream this *gnenpin* learned, too, that yellow was to be the favored color in the ceremony since it is the color of the sunrise and the most pleasing color to *Chau*. Consequently, animals of yellow color are offered—that is, if we have them."

Huenun now pulled from his saddlebag a small, badly worn, but precious old notebook. It had been given him by an old uncle who had written in it what he thought future generations of Araucanians should know. Huenun had shown us, on another day, the names of eighty-four caciques his uncle had written down and had said that they had been successive leaders of the *Mapuches* "from time that went very far back, indeed." Today he wanted to read to us what he himself had added at the dictation of his uncle—the uncle had grown too old to write. He read lines to himself in a whisper—they were written in Araucanian—and gave us the translations: Formerly, when clear skies and sunny weather were

71

needed, the cacique on the Pacific Coast called together the fathers of all the families under his jurisdiction, and they jointly decided on a day to hold a *gnillatun*. On the opening day, the father of every family brought with him a small amount of blue aniline dye, which he gave to the cacique's main helper—I shall call this helper captain. The men, Huenun interjected, took the blue dye from the supply that the women had on hand. He indicated the amount to be the size of his thumb from tip to base of nail. The women had traded the dye to peddlers who came among them, as they still do today. The dye, sometimes amounting to a kilogram, was sent to the cacique next in line on the way to the Cordillera. This cacique called together the fathers of families under him, and they, too, decided on a day to hold the *gnillatun*. Here again, on the opening day, every father brought a small amount of blue aniline dye. The cacique added theirs to the amount that had been sent to him, and sent all of it to the next cacique in line. The same was done by every cacique along the line until it reached the first cacique across the Cordillera. This is what was done when sunny weather and clear skies were needed.

If, on the other hand, there was a drought and rain was needed, a cacique from across the Cordillera instigated a series of *gnillatuns*. In place of blue aniline dye, tobacco was sent by the first cacique to the next one, and so all along the line until it reached the last cacique on the Pacific Coast. But instead of adding to the amount of tobacco, each cacique took a small portion from it. He had his *gnenpin* smoke it and blow the smoke skyward. Huenun concluded: "Blue dye is sent toward the Cordillera, because in that direction the sun rises and the skies are blue and clear; tobacco is sent toward the Pacific when rain is needed, because that is where the water is. Clear skies and sunny weather we call *kallful wenodagno*; rainy weather we call *kallfuchiwai*."

The manner in which he closed his little old notebook and replaced it almost reverently in his saddlebag made me think of how rare books are handled in our libraries; so did the scent of it.

"And now I shall tell you about the *gnillatun* itself. I have

72

A thatched ruka, *the traditional home of the Araucanians.*

Huenun Ñamku's handwriting. At left are the lines of a song in Araucanian; at right is the translation of the song in Spanish.

A scene at a gnillatun, *a religious ceremonial in which the Araucanians offer sacrifice and prayer to* Chau *(God) for a bountiful crop. Note the banners, pottery containing* mudai, *and smoke from the holy fire.*

Scene at a gnillatun. *Close-up of pottery containing* mudai.
Mudai *is an Araucanian alcoholic beverage which is today drunk
only at* gnillatuns, *and then not to intoxication.*

Volcano Lanín, "wearing a hat."

*Teresa, Huenun's daughter, wearing the traditional
Araucanian dress and silver jewelry.*

Huenun Ñamku's family and home. From left to right are three-year-old Rosamella, Jerónimo, Maríañuke, Maríañuke's mother, who is more than one hundred years old, Huenun, Lauriana, Maríañuke's sister, and twelve-year-old Hortensia.

Wooden plow made and used by Huenun in plowing his fields.

prepared what I am going to tell you. My wife, her mother, and I discussed it last evening; consequently, I can tell it well today, and it will not be necessary for you to ask me any questions." That meant no interruptions. Very well, Huenun!

And this is what he told: "Places in which the *gnillatun* is still conducted in Panguipulli area are Panguipulli, Calefquén, Huitag, Anacomoi, and Shoshuenco. Each cacique calls together the fathers of families under him, and together they decide on the day and place for the ceremonial—those who wish to make a sacrificial offering say so. Then all go home. (I have noticed that usually those who say they will offer a sacrifice are ones who have yellow animals. Yellow, as I told you before, signifies favorable weather for harvest time.) The *gnillatun* is usually conducted on the same pampa on which *gnillatuns* have always been conducted; that pampa is considered holy land. Ball games may be played on it, and cattle may graze there, but once a house is built on that pampa, it is no longer sacred ground.

"On the morning of the opening day, all families start from their homes, every man with a *pifülka* suspended from his neck. Men lead the animals to be sacrificed, and women follow with tortillas, *mudai*, and flour." A *pifülka*, Huenun explained, is a piece of wood or flat stone with one or several ventages at one end. Sounds are produced by blowing across the ventages much as a flute is played. *Mudai*, the traditional alcoholic beverage, is the product of fermented grain, and, as previously stated, is made by old women who chew kernels of grain or corn, spit them into a container, and allow them to ferment there. "Never, never," said Huenun in all earnestness, "is chicha drunk at the *gnillatun*, and never is *mudai* consumed by anyone to the state of intoxication." He was emphatic about this.

He continued: "The officiating persons at the *gnillatun* are two *gnenpins*—they are the cacique's helpers. I shall call these two captain and sergeant—the captain has more important duties than the sergeant. Then there are two highly respected old women, whom we call *pillañ kuche*, and two young girls. Today, a *machi* is some-

73

times asked to help, but that is probably because she can recall better than anyone else the details of the ceremonial, for she is one of the few who still lives almost entirely according to our old way and, therefore, remembers the old ways best. Formerly, no *machi* had anything to do with the *gnillatun*, absolutely nothing; she was present, but she was there just like all other persons."

The two young girls are chosen by one of the *gnenpins*. These girls must be old enough to ride a horse and know how to serve food, but young enough not to have entered womanhood. Sometimes the *gnenpin* chooses the daughters of the cacique and sometimes girls he has seen in a dream. He tells their parents about his choice. The parents are pleased and bring the girls to the holy pampa. When they come, each girl wears a blue sash.

While people are still arriving, the holy fire is built in the center of the pampa. Any boy or man may build it. Embers are fetched from the nearest *ruka*; the trunk of a dried apple tree is used as fuel. It is this fire that will consume the sacrificial animals. Food is cooked on fireplaces in family sun shelters just outside the holy pampa.

Huenun now produced from his saddlebag a diagram which he had prepared to use in telling us about the *gnillatun*. On it he had indicated the locations of activities and positions of participants. He pointed at these as he explained them. To the south, a short distance from the holy fire, the two old women sit, beating their *kultrugns* with drumsticks, and together singing songs to the rhythm. Women and children pick up the rhythm and dance around the two old women until four songs have been sung. Children who are not dancing are made to do so by the sergeant. At the *gnillatun* children often learn about self-control; parents, too, give them good advice. "I know now that I profited by the advice given me by my uncles at that time," said Huenun. "Children are also told at this time of the beginnings of their people: they are told that the first *Mapuches* grew from the earth, as grass does; that there was a well in which animals grew and from which they came forth; and similar important things, they are told."

74

At the end of the fourth song, every man locks his left arm with the right arm of a woman, and all dance in formation around the two old women, every man fifing his *pifülka* to the rhythm of the drumbeats. All dancing is done counterclockwise, and there is only one kind of dance. During this dance the captain and another man, both on horseback, each sway a banner attached to the tip of a long *colihüe* stalk, one banner blue, the other yellow. Today banners are made of cloth, but formerly women wove them of dyed yarn.

Francisca announced that it was time for dinner. After the customary siesta, Huenun continued: "I once heard it said that the *Mapuches* in Argentina imitate animals in their dances, but we on this side of the Cordillera do not dance that way." (During our study of the Argentine Araucanians in 1951–52, we found that he had been correctly informed.)

Huenun now sang, in Araucanian, three of the songs sung by the old women, and translated them—he did not know the fourth one. Each song, he said, consisted of repetitions of lines, and each line was sung in a different pitch. He began: "Number one: 'I was a volcano. I arrived at the volcano.' Number two: 'I want to chase away the wind that comes from the south. I want to send yellow clouds to the north.' " He explained, "Unfavorable weather for us here in Panguipulli comes from the south. This song really means to say that this wind that comes from the south, which is the one that does harm to our wheat, should go to the north. Number three: 'I come and am bringing two girls. Wind blow the clouds away.' When 'Wind blow the clouds away' is being sung, someone removes the blue sashes from the girls, and the sashes and the blue and yellow banners are waved. This signifies that favorable winds should blow away unfavorable weather."

He continued: Each girl now mounts a horse—one a white one, the other a yellow one—if a yellow horse is not available, a maroon will do. Small bells dangle from the bridles of the horses, and their haunches and necks are decorated in circles and blue diamond-shaped hatching—blue again signifying fair weather. The designs have no significance.

Each girl is now paired with one of the two men on horseback, and the four ride abreast, making an elliptical track which is to serve as a boundary line of the area within which all activities must take place. They ride the track four times, the men each swaying a banner. To the west of the holy fire are two men, each blowing a *trutruka*—any other man who has brought a *trutruka* is welcome to join them and blow his. The two men and the two girls terminate their rides south of the dancers, not far from the two old women. The men dismount and here set the *colihüe* stalks bearing the banners in the ground.

Now the sacrificial ceremonials begin. While the two old women beat their *kultrugn*, the sergeant hands a yellow hen and a pipe filled with tobacco to the captain—pipes at the *gnillatun* must be of wood or clay. The hen has been resting near the place where the banners were set; the pipe was there, also. The captain, holding the hen by the feet and swinging it skyward, says a prayer of petition: he prays for favorable weather, for an abundant harvest, for health for the people and their animals, for an increase in animals, and for whatever else he wishes. After the prayers are said, the sergeant breaks the neck of the hen or tears off her head, drops her on the ground, and sits by until she has died, drawing drafts from the pipe and blowing smoke skyward. The sergeant now throws the hen on the holy fire where it is completely consumed. If anyone else has brought a hen to be sacrificed, it, too, has been killed and may now be thrown on the fire.

Next, sheep and calves and maybe a young horse, which have all been hitched nearby until now, are prepared for sacrifice. There are two ways in which the blood of these animals may be offered: the animal may be killed and the blood squeezed from the heart and sprinkled about, or the pulsating heart of the living animal may be pulled forward and the blood allowed to squirt about at each pulsation. In either case, the captain holds the heart for all to see, while he prays, "Hear us, *Chau*! We are all united in this prayer. Hear us, Father in the far above and woman with him. Hear us! Give us blue skies so that we shall have a good harvest."

76

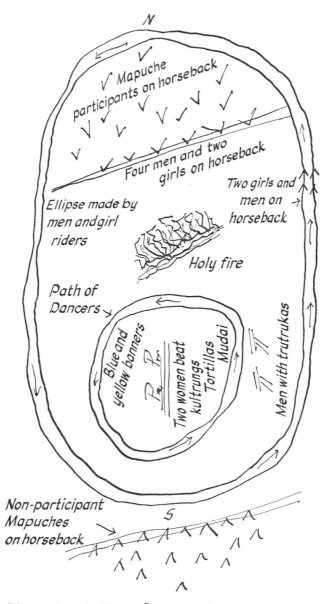

Diagram drawn by Huenun Ñamku showing locations of participants
and activities at the *gnillatun*.

"Today," added Huenun, "many families sacrifice only hens because they are poorer than formerly. However, as poor as I am, I sacrificed a calf six years ago after my eldest daughter had died— she was the seventh of my children to die. A *machi* told me that someone was doing me harm and that my remaining children and my wife would also die; already the evil with which to kill them had been prepared. She said that if I offered a calf at the *gnillatun*, their deaths might be averted. I offered the calf. My wife and children are all living."

While the large animal is being consumed by the holy fire, every father walks around it and dashes a pinch of flour into the fire. He may do this as often as he is moved to do so, and each time he does, he prays *Chau* to bring to a favorable harvest all that the people have planted. After the men have made their offerings, mothers of families are invited to do the same, but only those come forward who have brought flour with them and who have an inclination to offer some—usually these are only old women. No children are permitted to participate in this ceremonial. While the flour is being offered, the captain, smoking the pipe and blowing smoke skyward, begs *Gnünechén* to grant favorable weather and an increase in animals. He prays also that families, especially those participating in the *gnillatun*, be maintained in good health and that sickness bypass them and go elsewhere. After this, all again dance as before, but this time around the stalks with the banners.

And now the caciques—or if there is only one present, he and some of the older men—meet to the north of the fire and encourage each other to keep intact the customs of their forefathers; they make it a point to say that they are doing so right now by celebrating the *gnillatun*. They then ask God to bless crops and families. "There is really much talking going on among them," said Huenun. "It is not unusual for them to talk for an hour. We sometimes wonder what they are talking about." Following this, the captain prays again while the cacique and people stand by in close formation.

Next, two men on horseback, each with a *trutruka*, take position to the north of the holy fire; the captain and one of the two

78

girls are mounted on horses to the right of them; the other man and girl, also on horses, to the left. These six now stand in line facing the holy fire. Back of them and also facing the fire, are all other participants who came on horseback. The sergeant now rides back and forth, four times, in front of the line of six, each time ordering all to yell "*Ya-ah!*" All nonparticipants—usually these have come as observers or with old persons who participate—arrange themselves in similar formation to the south of the fire, but outside the ellipse—nonparticipants never enter the ellipse. "These are invited *Mapuches*," Huenun explained. "No gringos or *Chilenos blancos* are ever allowed to be present—only invited *Mapuches* are permitted there." After the "*Ya-ah!*" has been yelled, the line of six exchanges position with those on horseback who are behind them. This exchange of positions takes place four times; each time, when it is completed, the sergeant rides back and forth and exhorts all to yell "*Ya-ah!*" With this the ceremonial ends.

Women now leave for the sunshelters—each family or several together have erected one outside and to the east of the ellipse. Participating men and boys seat themselves in a semicircle where the banners are standing, that is, within the ellipse to the south and west. Women serve them *mudai* and toasted wheat here, and sometimes tortillas and roasted meat, also. Invited men and boys, nonparticipants, go to the sun shelters to eat; all women and girls eat there, also.

After all have eaten, the *konchatun* is performed; it is an integral part of the *gnillatun* and should never be performed except at the *gnillatun*, and then only after the meal. Huenun was emphatic about this. The *konchatun* takes place in the northeast part of the ellipse, where all gather.

At the *konchatun*, Huenun continued, one man reciprocates an act of friendship another man rendered him at some time. These two men stand facing each other; if they wish it, another man may stand alongside each of them. The reciprocating man cuts a sheep completely open at the underside, from neck downward, takes out the heart and, while it still pulsates, hands it to his friend, express-

79

ing words of gratitude to God for having granted him the good fortune of having this man as his friend. The two together then flip some blood of the sheep skyward and toward the holy fire. Following this, the reciprocating man gives the slaughtered sheep to his friend, who cuts off the head and right front leg and asks someone present—probably the man who has been standing by his side, if there has been one—to take the remainder of the sheep and put it in his (the recipient's) sun shelter. Later the recipient takes it home. From then on these two friends stay close to each other until all depart for home. Huenun seemed to like the *konchatun*, and regretted that in recent years it is sometimes omitted at the *gnillatun*. "Our young men do not want to learn how to perform it," he said in slightly angry tones. "Eventually it will die out. I am glad you are recording what I tell you, because I know that what I tell you is the truth. It is most important that generations of *Mapuches* yet to be born can learn the truth.

"By now evening has come," Huenun went on to say. "All prepare to leave for home, but before doing so, there is a grand finale. All men who came on horseback ride around the elliptical track four times, while those with *pifülkas* fife them, those with *trutrukas* blow them, the two old women beat their *kultrugns*, and every man, woman, and child fills the air with '*Ya-ah's!*' "

At the very end, *mudai* is put into a pottery vessel and is buried where the banners are planted. "Now," said Huenun with enthusiasm, "at the next *gnillatun*—maybe in a year or two, or three or four, although there should be one every year—this container will be unearthed, and if the *mudai* has turned to kernels of wheat or corn or if it is still in liquid form, it is a good sign and indicates that we shall have a fruitful year. If it has turned to earth or has disappeared, it is a sign that we shall have a bad year."

Margaret wanted to ask him if he had ever seen either of these happen. That was her primary question. Her second was, "Did he himself really believe what he had just said?" These and many other questions remained unanswered for the time. Huenun was not to be our last informant, we knew. We were sincerely grateful to him for his detailed, well-prepared account of the religious ceremonial of his people, and we would not hurt him by interrupting him.

"Should it happen," added Huenun, "that so many animals are brought for sacrifice as to warrant a second day of ceremonials, the sergeant wakes at the holy fire all night to keep it smoldering. Families who live close by go home, but those who have come from far stay in nearby *rukas*. All make their appearance again the following morning for a repetition of the ceremonials. Every day the ceremonials are the same as the first day. I have attended *gnillatuns* that have lasted five days," he added.

"The last day of the ceremonial must end when the sun is there [at an angle of forty-five degrees] because the people have to be home before dark since there is always danger of attacks by pumas after dark. And I must go home now, too. I am glad that I had this opportunity to tell you about our religion. Our people should continue to conduct the *gnillatun* even though we are now Christians. Everything is becoming worse and worse for the *Mapuches*. I myself have a longing to instigate a *gnillatun* once more. I want to ask *Chau* to give me a good supply of grain just once again. I should like once more to feel free of worry. I plan to ask the cacique to conduct one."

I expressed to Huenun my high regard for his excellent account of the *gnillatun*. Margaret told him that he deserved this expression of appreciation unreservedly. He thanked us for the sack of grain we gave him. Margaret and I accompanied him to the door, watched him mount his horse, and waved *adiós* to him as he rode away.

I felt pensive, as I have often felt after an old person, especially one of another culture, has told me of an old custom, precious to him, that was passing out of his life. "American Indians are not pagans," I said to Margaret. "These people have a firm belief in God, in God as both creator and maintainer. Their tribal religious ceremonial is to them an expression of that inner conviction that man has that there is a Being greater than himself, One on Whom he can call when life's problems need solutions other than those

81

that he, as man, can find." Huenun was sad. He needed a more fruitful harvest to feed his family. The prayers of the *gnillatun* might bring him the blessings of his fields, he thought. His horse seemed to sense Huenun's unsolved problem, for it walked slowly with head drooping—other days we had seen it gallop away in high spirits. We watched Huenun disappear behind the foothills of Villarrica. Margaret closed the door. Another day had ended.

CHAPTER VIII

Huenun's Wife and Daughter

We had a most pleasant surprise today. Huenun brought his wife and one of his daughters. "This is Maríañuke, my wife," he said as he presented her, "and this is my daughter." Since our delight at meeting was mutual, our handshaking and the *koyaqtun* were really sincere and heartfelt. Huenun seemed glad to have his wife and daughter with him. They presented us with ears of corn and bouquets of garden flowers. "This is *Mapuche* corn," Huenun said, pointing at some ears; "it has both blue and white kernels. This variety, which matures early, we call *tralawopi*. This kind [pointing at other ears] has only white kernels; we call it maize, as the Chileans do; we have no *Mapuche* word for it." From this we inferred that maize was not a pre-European food in the Araucanian country. Huenun then called our attention to the traditional silver ornaments worn by his wife and daughter and the manner in which they had dressed their hair. "Old customs with us," he added.

Before Francisca could fetch more chairs, Huenun had stepped over the school benches that Francisca had shoved to one side and lifted from behind them a small bench. He placed it alongside the school benches and, after brushing the dust off it with his hat, sat down on it, motioning to his wife and daughter to sit beside him. While Huenun was arranging things, I beamed at Margaret: "Now, I am certain, we shall have an opportunity to learn some customs about children."

Our study was to be primarily an ethnological one of child life. I had not succeeded in getting such information at a previous interview with Huenun. On this day I had asked him how an Araucanian child learns to walk. "Does it do so by itself," I asked, "or must it be taught to do so?" He became annoyed. I thought I had asked a question in which any father would be interested. I could have asked him about the care of the umbilical cord or what was used as talcum powder for the baby or what was used for diapers. But I knew I was exercising good judgment not to ask him these questions. Also, I might hurt him, something I most certainly did not want to do. However, I needed to know the answers for a complete study of child life. After Huenun's obvious annoyance at my question, I decided to ask only women for information related to small children. Mothers on the coastal range had been interested in anything pertaining to babies.

Although he had been annoyed, he did answer my question. The child's mother makes a gangway by staking two rows of quila poles (*Muehlenbeckia sagittifolia*) a half arm-stretch apart—rows are two arm-stretches in length. To each row she ties a pole horizontally. Then she teaches the child to stand up holding on to the horizontal poles, and coaxes him to come to her by moving along the gangway. He watched Margaret write down these details as I dictated them to her. When he saw she had finished, he blurted out, "I am not flattered by being asked these unimportant questions about babies! I do not think that all this about babies has any value. Let us talk about something that requires intelligence. What else do you wish to know?"

This incident had occurred a few days ago. Today we had Maríañuke to ask. Our problem was how to get her to answer questions in the presence of Huenun. "Why should a woman talk when there is a man around to do so," we had been told by women on the coastal range, but we had learned that when no man was present, these same women were jovial conversationalists and excellent informants.

We had learned, too, that a woman rarely speaks to a stranger in the presence of a man. I hoped that Huenun's wife, however, would, in due time, talk to us. I continued with Huenun. "Here's a question, Huenun, that I am certain both you and your wife can answer. To answer it requires intelligence, I think." What I wanted to know was how a child learns the Araucanian language. I thought leading to it indirectly would be a wise approach. "How," I said, "can Margaret and I learn the *Mapuche* language?"

"Just like you learn any other language," replied Huenun. "Find someone who knows *Mapuche*, and have him write words for you and tell you what they mean; learn to pronounce these words and keep on pronouncing them correctly—memorize them. *Señorita* Margarita will not have much trouble pronouncing them, but you will; you seem to have difficulty whenever you pronounce one, I have noticed. Then, after you know many words, associate with *Mapuches* who speak only *Mapuche*. Since there are two old women in my home who speak only *Mapuche*, you may stay with us and learn from them. You will be forced, then, to form sentences with your words. I invite you to come and live with us for a while, and after you are able to speak *Mapuche*, you can get one of those books that the Capuchin fathers have written—the ones that have *Mapuche* and Spanish sentences. Read these, and write them. I shall give you one lesson now. Write down these words: *ügnüm*— it means 'bird'; *küllwi*—it means 'beans'; *allfida*, 'peas'; *ponon*, 'lungs'; *makuñ*, 'poncho'; *piuke*, 'heart'. There, that is one lesson."

This reminded him of the manner in which he and the German Capuchin priest, Father Félix José de Augusta, had compiled a two-volume dictionary, *Diccionario Araucano-Español*, and a second volume, *Diccionario Español-Araucano*.[1] Félix José had little cards upon each of which a Spanish word was written. To each Spanish word he added its equivalent in Araucanian and its meaning as Huenun told it. The Araucanian words he wrote according to the phonetic sounds of the German language, but since some of the Araucanian phonetic sounds had no German equivalents, he devised symbols for these with the help of Huenun's pronunciation. For

[1] Published in Santiago, Chile, in 1916.

example, he symbolized the phonetic sound of *gn* in German by an *n* with a hook; an inverted *e* is pronounced like a German *u*, with some force and from the throat, like gargling without water—it is written *ü*; *l'*, *n'* and *t'* are pronounced with the tip of tongue between nearly closed teeth. In the present study we are using these equivalents: *gn*, as in *gnillatun* (religious ceremonial); *ü*, as in *pifülka* (fife); *l'*, as in *l'uan* (constellation).

On another set of cards Huenun had written Araucanian words, and for each word Félix José added its meaning, the equivalent word in Spanish, and the pronunciation as Huenun spoke it. At a later time Félix José also collected words in other areas where Araucanians live, and dialect differences showed up. After Huenun had helped to resolve these, Félix José indicated them in the *Diccionarios*: for example, words used only in Panguipulli are preceded by an asterisk; those used only in Huapi, by a cross. Huenun now walked to a corner of the room where we had our books, cameras, and other equipment stored and returned with volume one of the *Diccionarios*; turning to page xiv, he pointed at his name, given there as an authority on pronunciation of the Araucanian language. He looked at his name and then remarked, "It is printed here as 'Huenuñamco', but it should be 'Huenun Ñamku.' In your book call me 'Huenun Ñamku.' "

He continued: "We also compiled a grammer, and this took us a year. We two, Father Félix José and I, always worked together." Father Sigifredo had told us earlier that the Jesuit fathers had compiled a dictionary and had written a grammer in both Araucanian and Spanish as early as 1605, that this much was known, but that every attempt to find them had been futile. It is a matter of record that the Jesuit fathers came to Chile in 1593.

Huenun continued, "After we completed the dictionaries and the grammer, I taught Father Sigifredo the *Mapuche* language—I taught him as I told you to learn it. He found the pronunciation a little difficult, just about as much as you do. I also helped Father Atanasio, another German Capuchin, to collect insects and plants, and I told him the *Mapuche* names for them. We did the work here

86

in Panguipulli. That was eighteen or twenty years ago, and Father Atanasio has died since. Two years ago, two men from Santiago asked Father Sigifredo to help them find a potato-like root that we call *mawida poñü*, or *ñangki* [*Dioscorea nervosa*] and use to bleach cloth white. Father Sigifredo asked me to find it for them, and I did. The men promised to send me some compensation, but as yet I have not received it.

"When you are learning the *Mapuche* language, you will have to learn words, too, that we borrowed from the Chileans to describe things for which we had no *Mapuche* names. For example, since we had no oats or name for oats, we adopted the Chilean word *avena*, which means oats. Since we have always had grain like wheat, we use our own word, *kachilla*, for wheat and not the Chilean word, *trigo*. For horse we say *kawell*, which is very much like the Chilean word *caballo*. For hog we say *sanchu*; we should say *chanchu*, as Chileans do, but sometimes we find it difficult to pronounce Chilean words as Chileans do, and so we pronounce them our own way. [Margaret thought that it might be opportune to tell him right now that for the same reason I found it difficult at times to pronounce *Mapuche* words as *Mapuches* do.] Some *Mapuche* words have changed since former times: for example, a very long time ago an olla was called a *dügnoll*; today we say *challa*."

We had been told by a non-Araucanian that Araucanian women have a language which they speak exclusively among themselves. "Is this correct?" I asked, directing my question to Maríañuke.

Huenun answered, "How could we understand them, if they did? Women may have secrets, certainly, which they whisper to each other or walk away from the crowd to tell each other, but they will say whatever they are saying to each other in the ordinary *Mapuche* language. Or it may happen that a woman sings a song in such a way that bystanders cannot understand what she is singing, but she is not singing it in any language except the *Mapuche* language. For instance, there is a song that a woman sings when she grinds grain on her metate; she sings it to herself—my wife sings it. I do not understand her words; in fact, I seldom listen to her singing. One song she sings, I know, is about the eagle: the eagle is disgusted and flies away to another land without saying farewell. However, she sings it in *Mapuche* words."

He then expressed regret at not having had an opportunity for formal education, such as young Araucanians have today. "I never had an opportunity to go to school," he lamented, "but one of my relatives did. He had studied in Valdivia, and had a first reader in Spanish. He would point at words in it and tell me their meaning and how to pronounce them. Then I would pronounce them as he did and repeat what he had said they meant. After that I would repeat them to myself wherever I would be. During the rainy season he let me have the book. It had lessons on the eye, the hand, the parrot, and other subjects, with a picture of each; under each picture there was writing. In the evening I would lie on my back near the fireplace with the book in my hands and read the sentences to myself. This relative also taught me how to use my hands to write. I observed his hands as he wrote letters and words in the ashes of the fireplace—he used a little stick to do so. I imitated him and wrote them as he did; I wrote these words in ashes wherever I found any dumped. I also wrote words on fungus, the fungus that grows on trees around here; it is white and soft, and we call it *lupekonükon*. Sometimes I wrote on the inner side of bark of dead trees—if a tree has been dead for sometime, it is not difficult to write on the inner side of its bark. We had no paper in those days, nor pencils."

Francisca added that children today use fungi and the inner bark of trees on which to write—homework is sometimes handed in on it—she noted that paper is scarce in mountain villages and cash is needed to buy it. "Not many *Mapuches* have cash on hand," she added.

Huenun continued: "I had already learned how to write my name when people were saying the time had arrived for a change in the presidency of Chile. We were all to vote. The wife of a Chilean taught me how to write my name; she wrote it for me, and I practiced writing it. That helped. After some time I had to go to Cuícui

88

to inscribe my name in the Registry of Voters. I voted for Pedro Mott and was paid ten pesos for it. Pedro Mott was elected president that time."

Maríañuke and the daughter were listening to our conversation. We occasionally exchanged smiles; we understood that we had good will toward each other. I did so very much wish to ask Maríañuke some questions, but, as I have already stated, I had learned that women rarely talk to strangers in the presence of men. Margaret was eager for me to get started, but I was not sure how to begin. I complimented Huenun on bringing his wife and said that I believed she must be an intelligent person. (I had noticed her quick, intelligent glances, her delicate manners, and her fine features.) I went on to say that I could now better understand what both Francisca and Father Sigifredo had meant when they told us that his, Huenun's, children were all well bred, had acceptable manners, and were respectable persons. I went on to say that undoubtedly his wife had been a great help to him in rearing his children, that it seemed to me that she would be able to tell us her part in it, and that I would like to ask her some questions. Would he permit it?

He replied, looking with sympathetic love toward her, "My wife does not get out much, and she is seldom among people; consequently, she is reserved and speaks little. In fact, she does not know much."

We had read in early travelers' accounts that Araucanian women held an inferior position in the eyes of Araucanian men and that, in instances, they were slaves to their men. We had not found this to be true on the coastal range. Huenun's estimate of his wife recalled this to my mind. I asked him, "Do you like and esteem your wife?"

Promptly he replied, "I most certainly do! I most certainly like her. Anyway, that is the way it should be. We are married; it is our duty to love each other."

His wife, with a look of surprise, at once followed up his statement with, "Most certainly do we like each other. I like him, too. We are married; it is understood that we like each other. It sometimes happens that a couple is not well matched, and then they are both unhappy. But we have always been happy together." These were Mariañuke's first words directed to us.

Although she had now spoken to us, I was quite certain that Huenun, and not she, would answer my questions, and it was he who wanted no questions related to babies. Consequently, I asked some questions related to older children. "How," I asked, "do parents teach their children the right and wrong of things?"

"Parents take time out to instruct and counsel their children," he answered. "When my grandfather told my uncle, the one who reared me, that I had done something wrong, my uncle would talk to me about it and tell me not to do it again, and, I obeyed him. I have done the same for my children; I talk to them if they have done something wrong, but I talk to them just once. If they fail in something serious, I will probably inject a warning, but I shall warn them only once. Then, if that child fails in the same thing a second time, I spank him. I have treated our girls in the same way; that is, they are dealt with in this manner when they are small and not yet going to school. Once children go to school, they need no longer be punished in this way—at least not my children. When somebody in our valley did something very wrong when I was a child, my grandmother or my uncle would talk to me and tell me not to do anything like that, and I have done the same for my children. Then, too, my grandmother talked to me during her leisure time. She would say to me, 'Always behave well. Grow up to be a good man. Have good will toward all people.' "

Huenun thought that reasonable allowance should be made for a child's misconduct. "However, if an order has been given," he added, "it should be obeyed at once." His wife acquiesced. He continued: "For example, if my wife sends a child some place to do something, and the child does not go because he is afraid to go there, my wife has sympathy for the child and goes there and does it herself. That is her way of doing. But if I give a child an order and he says that he is afraid to go, I threaten to punish him if he does not go. That is my way of doing."

90

I then asked, "Is a child ever punished by being deprived of food?"

His wife, astounded at this question, answered immediately with dismay—I had directed the question to Huenun—"Punish a child by depriving him of food? No! No! Most certainly not that way. Who could do such a thing? Are there really people who will deprive a child of food for any reason whatsoever? A child has hunger like everybody else, and he has a right to food. If a child needs to be punished, he should be slapped or spanked and, if necessary, with a leather strap."

Huenun made no comment, but continued: "A small child may resist wearing clothes—small children seldom wear any—and will try to tear them off; he will lie on the floor and yell and kick. I would teach that child to behave by spanking him right then, but his mother would take that child in her arms, talk to him, and try to pacify him. She has much patience with a small child; however, as soon as the child walks, she, too, will punish him. She may even slap him with a leather strap," and added somewhat amused, "but she will fold the strap to make it short so it will not sting too much! I have seen my wife spank a child who soiled himself with feces and another who played in the mud. I have never whipped a small child; it is really the mother's duty to rear a small child. When the child is older, the mother does not have the heart to whip him, and then the father must do so."

I then asked some leading questions about stealing, to which Huenun answered: "If a child steals, he is whipped as soon as the parents hear about it, and then he is given earnest advice not to steal again; he is emphatically told that stealing makes trouble for himself and others. My grandfather told me, on several occasions, that formerly a child who stole was taught an unforgettable lesson —he learned never to steal again. An older person set a rat's nest on fire—rats, you know, steal too—and held the child's hand in the fire."

His wife, greatly surprised at this, said in a disapproving voice, "How could anyone have done that? Certainly they would only hold his hands in the smoke of the fire; they would most certainly not burn a child's hands intentionally!"

Huenun listened to her, but went on, "When I caught one of our boys lying, I reprimanded him. I warned him not to lie again and said that if he lied again, I would whip him. I said the same to our girls. Generally, a child who is scolded or whipped goes to his grandmother's *ruka* to be consoled, but that is all right, for the grandmother, too, will tell him to behave himself, but in a sympathetic way. If the child has no grandmother living nearby, he will stay around home and be ashamed of himself—this is good for him, too. Children should sometimes think about themselves and about what they have done; this is a good time to do it."

At this point I asked him to tell of an occasion when he himself had lied and what had happened. He laughed heartily, and said, "I will tell no stories on myself, stories about lying!" However, he did tell the following: "When I was about fifteen years old, my father's sisters put my cousin and me up to stealing a sheep—my cousin was probably twenty years old. We did so, and I carried the sheep home on my back. We stole it because we had had nothing to eat for nearly a week. Although it was not our custom to steal, we were hungry and had to find food somewhere. I was not punished for this, but I would have been if I had stolen without permission. My grandmother, too, knew we had stolen the sheep, and we always thought that the people from whom we had stolen that sheep suspected us, but they never obliged us to pay it back. Maybe they knew that we had been hungry for a long time.

"A child that steals should be punished," he went on to say, "unless, as I indicated, he steals because he is hungry and has no food. Not far from us is a mestizo: his father is a *Mapuche*; his mother, a Chilean. He stole when he was small, but was never punished. As he grew older, he stole whenever he had an opportunity; he even stole a hat from a man sleeping on the roadside, once. Recently, he stole six hundred pesos from a sleeping man, but he was apprehended while trying to pay for a hat, pants, and a pair of shoes with some of that money. He is now locked up by the Chilean police that come around here."

"How did you train a child not to be jealous?" I asked. I suggested that maybe he would let his wife tell us about it.

He was annoyed at this and said, "She? How can she answer it? I told you that she really does not know much; she seldom leaves home." I was not certain that he comprehended the meaning of the word jealousy and gave an example. He responded, "If a girl is jealous of her sister because her sister has been given something which she herself is not given, the mother will simply tell her to quiet herself and she will be given the same thing, eventually."

I then asked, "If one of two brothers had a cow and the other did not, would the one brother be jealous of the other?"

"No," he answered. "Anyway, my sons never had a cow each."

We had heard on the coastal range that a personality prediction test is given to boys. To check the information, I asked Huenun whether he had ever heard it said that a boy whose voice is changing is given chicha until he is completely intoxicated and that his parents observe his conduct when he is in this condition and predict from it what kind of man he will become. "We do not wait until his voice changes," he replied; "sometimes a boy's voice does not change until he is fifteen or maybe twenty years old. We test a boy when he is much, much younger than that. My wife's eldest sister tested her eldest son this way, but his conduct did not turn out according to prediction, and this was a disappointment; consequently, she did not test her other sons. However, it is not chicha that we use; it is the seeds of *miyaiya* [probably Jimson weed; *Datura stramonium*]. Since I wanted to test my sons, I planted *miyaiya* seeds in my garden, but the plants were choked by other plants. *Miyaiya* seeds are very small; they are like the seeds of garden peas when they are just beginning to form."

I now asked how a child received his name. Huenun began, "A child is given his name when he is still small, and this is his name for life. There are *Mapuche* names that are given only to girls, and

there are *Mapuche* names that are given only to boys. It is like this:
When we baptize a girl today, we call her María; if it is a boy, we
call him Mário. Now, no one would think of the person named
Mário as being a girl. In the same way, if we hear a person called
Licanrayen, we know that she is a woman; if someone speaks of
Licankura, we know that he is speaking of a man. I do not know how
Mapuche names originated, but those that are at present bestowed
by parents on their children have been used in the family for a long
time. Many *Mapuche* names have meanings; some have not." He
then wrote the following feminine names and gave their meanings:
Nümeipan—*pan* is an abbreviated form of *pangui*, which means
lion; the name means "someone-who-took-the-lion." Hualtuipan
means "lion-that-is-enclosed." Licanrai means "stone-flower," for
lican means stone, and *rai* is a shortened form of *rayen*, which
means flower. Llanquirai means "witchcraft-stone-with-flower."
Pinsha means "hummingbird." Laftuipan means "running-lion."
Then he wrote some feminine names that did not lend themselves
to translation: Pushmei, Llefllai, Pinshalrai, and Penshoria. "There
now! All *Mapuches* know that these names are given to women;
now I shall write some names given to men: Wentamui, Lifkelai,
Küpainau, and Wiliñanco. And that is enough for names. What is
your next question?"

I asked him to listen while I read the following statement from
a book[2] written by Félix José de Augusta:

> There are women, in truth, who have no names, although this is rare;
> or maybe had one, but forgot it, since it was so seldom used. In the
> *Mapuche* language the words indicating relationships are so definite
> and so distinctly different that for the woman who does not partici-
> pate in public or civil life it is not necessary to use another name.

In a tone of vexation Huenun spouted, "Certainly, most certainly,
did women have names! There were names for men and names for
women, as I just told you." I continued to read:

> Since women do not participate in public or in civil life, a woman's

2 *Como Se Llaman Los Araucanos* (Padre las Casas, Chile, 1907), 38–39.

94

personal name is used very little, only if the missionary must have it to record it in a book; hardly anyone else asks for her name. Or maybe it is because the woman is looked upon as an object which is bought by the man and sold by the father of the family. Generally, one needs to beg the woman to tell her name. Women worry that they will be laughed at by others who ridicule them from motives that we sometimes do not know.[3]

At this Huenun was indignant. "First of all," he began, "women did not have to be ashamed of their names. If a man is called upon to speak at a gathering of the people at which speeches are made, the person calling him will say, 'So and so, son of such a man,' giving the personal names of the man and of his father. Now, the idea that the woman had no name in the early days may have come from the fact that a woman was never called upon to speak in public; a woman, therefore, never had to have her name pronounced so that everyone heard it—she did not have to be called on as the daughter of such-and-such a man. Women had nothing to do in public life, but every woman had a name. Nor have I ever heard of a woman who had a name that she did not like to have others pronounce. How could I know the names of my grandmother and other women if I had not heard them spoken? They were not ashamed of their names. Everybody knew my grandmother's name, Mañke-kura; it meant 'stone-of-a-condor'; one of my mother's sisters was called Kallfü, 'blue', and another, Llanka, which is best translated as meaning 'magic-stone.' Names of other women of my mother's age that I can recall right now were Hufitrai, Huispu, Kurüi, and my mother's name was Kallfukar. Now, should it happen that a woman forgets her name because she says she never hears it spoken, it is a sign that such a woman lacks intelligence. There were such women!"

I remarked, "I am wondering what Father Félix José would say if he had just heard you."

"Father Félix was surprised at me for knowing so much," he retorted; "he said this more than once while I was helping him

3 *Ibid.*, 38–39.

with the *Diccionarios*. I am surprised at myself for knowing so much about the things you want to know and for being able to answer your questions, and I am surprised, too, that you are so intelligent and know so much about the things you are asking me about."

He sat silent for a while, seeming to think, then conferred with his wife and daughter in Araucanian, and continued, "Maybe the reason why a woman does not hear her name pronounced for a long time is because of a custom that we have by which the mother's name is seldom used in the family. When the first child is born, the mother is no longer called by her personal name. For example, when my first child was born, we baptized her María. From then on my wife was called Maríañuke, which means 'María's mother.' Always the name of the first-born is placed before the word for mother, *ñuke*. The same is true with regard to the father. After María was born, I was called Maríagnichau, which means 'María's father.' Since I was the eldest in my family, my mother was always called Huenunñuke. However, only members of one's family such as one's grandparents and the brothers and sisters of one's father and mother, use these terms. When the second child is born, there is no change in the names of the parents; parents are always known by the name of their first-born child, even when they have the status of grandparents. If the first child dies, however, the parents again take their own given names."

With great care now he read the feminine names listed by Félix José. "Judging from the meanings of these names," he explained, "they must have been collected on the Pacific Coast." He translated some: Antutray, "cascade-of-the-sun"; Apoil′eufu, "river-that-filled-itself"; Amuinera, "a-fox-that-has-left"; Aye-lewei, "laughing"; Aflai, "who-is-not-finished"; Allwekintui, "sought-with-interest"; Ayunkew, "a-loved-land-of-stone"; Kall-furay, "blue flower"; Kinturay, "she-who-looks-for-flowers"; Liftuipani, "a-puma-who-washes"; Llankuray, "a-flower-that-has-dropped-off."

His daughter had gone out to check their horses—they had

come on horseback. On her return she said to Huenun that the sun was nearly touching the Cordillera. Another day was coming to an end. We had had a pleasant interview and had enjoyed being together. Huenun's wife was particularly pleased with our dinner, a delicious lamb stew, and the coffeetime snack, hot coffee and apple-centered cinnamon rolls which the sisters had served us.

"Would you like to have your pictures taken?" I asked. Huenun answered that he would be grateful indeed to have them taken and to have prints of them. We stepped into favorable sunlight, and I photographed them. Huenun was contented with the kilos of flour we gave him and several large red handkerchiefs brought from North America. Maríañuke and her daughter were pleased with bags of yerba maté and a set of earrings for each which we had also brought from North America.

At parting, Maríañuke extended a warm invitation for us to visit them in their home and to meet there her old mother who lived with them. We promised to do this. Francisca, Margaret, and I accompanied them to where their horses were grazing—now neighing. We waved *adiós* and watched them until they disappeared behind the hills. We wondered again at the courtesy and refined manners of Araucanian women, and we looked forward to interviews with women in the secluded higher valleys of the Andes.

CHAPTER IX

Marriage in the Araucanian Way

It was a bright morning, and Huenun arrived exactly on time. His handshaking was wholehearted; the *koyaqtun*, most friendly. Margaret settled herself at the end of the table. "How can you tell time so exactly, Huenun?" she asked.

"When the sun is out, I have no difficulty doing so," he answered, "but when there is no sun, I can make only a guess. What time does your watch say it is? Exactly nine? Well then, let us begin." And he took his accustomed place at the table.

He began, "Now that you have been asking me about our old customs, many come vividly to my mind. Today I shall tell you about our marriage customs, and what I tell you is strictly an old custom. In the higher valleys of the Cordillera they still marry this way, but very few people in our valley do so; however, you will find such marriages in Coñaripe Valley. This custom should be of particular interest to Margarita," he added, pushing his eyebrows forward, "for she is still a *señorita*; to you it is only something to record as another *Mapuche* custom."

He stepped to the window to satisfy himself that his horse was grazing where he had left it and then began energetically: "A father decides that his son is to marry. He may then discuss the matter with his son or ask another man to do so; usually he asks another man. This done, the father or the go-between goes to the father of the girl whom he wants his son to marry to see what he thinks of it. If both fathers are satisfied, they discuss the price to be paid for the girl and come to an agreement in regard to the number and kinds of animals that are to be paid. Generally, the bride price consists of one or more horses, several cows, and several sheep.

"The mother of the girl has the right to express her opinion and has been known to say, 'I do not want to give my child to that man; I do not know him.' But if the father of the girl thinks he is the right man for his daughter, he can make all arrangements without his wife's consent. That has happened. It has happened, too, that the girl's mother still objects when the man and his relatives come to fetch the bride, but if the girl herself does not protest, her mother's objections are overruled. The young man's mother, too, has the right to discuss the pros and cons of the marriage of her son; she may even ask someone, who can speak well and more convincingly than she, to talk to her son. But the two fathers make the decision and set the day for the marriage. While waiting for the day to arrive, the father of the groom invites men, sometimes women also, usually all relatives, to go with him to the home of the girl on the appointed day. There may be as many as thirty guests, who take with them the bride price. I myself was one of such a group four times, and I know from those experiences how this is done. Each time the man's father invited me. One time, I recall, we were twenty mature men, two young men, and one old woman—they needed that many men to drive all the cattle being taken as the bride price. The old woman was asked to go because she was an able speaker; she was to give advice to the prospective bride. The man to be wed goes along, of course, but he stays in the background.

"Now the day for the marriage has come, and the girl does not know that the men are coming. To make certain that she will be home when they arrive, they leave very early in the morning—in fact, early enough that they will be sure to arrive before the girl can possibly have left home for the fields or gardens or wherever she may be going. When the men arrive, they stealthily surround the *ruka* that is the girl's home so that she can be caught if she attempts to run away. Each animal in the bride price is tied to a separate lasso, and the father of the bridegroom stands holding the ends of them, ready to hand them to the father of the bride, one by one, when the appropriate time comes.

"As I have said, the men and women have now arrived and have encircled the *ruka*. After the *koyaqtun* between the two fathers, the father of the groom says, 'I have come to bring you these animals,' and he names them one by one. 'I have brought them to you so that you will give me your daughter for my son.' Then he gives the reason why he has chosen this man's daughter; his reason may be her good character, her breeding, her good behavior, her beauty, or for whatever other reason he has wanted this particular girl for his son. He will end by saying, 'I beg of you to give me this daughter.'

"Then the father of the bride speaks. He says, 'It is true, I have reared my child well, but I did not do this because I thought that you would come to ask for her. If I give you my child, it is because I know you; I know who you are.' Or he may say that he is giving his daughter to him because he knows his father or his brothers, or because he is a relative, or because he is someone whom he knows very, very well. Whatever his reason is, he will state it. Then the young man's father hands the lassos to the girl's father, one by one. If the girl's father is satisfied, he says, 'I accept them. I give you my child.'

"The sentence, 'I give you my child,' " Huenun went on to say, "is the most important one of all, for it obliges the young woman to go with the man. After it has been spoken, the bride is given good advice by her parents. They will tell her to go with the young man and to be a good wife to him; they will also tell her that she should not run away from him, that she should be well behaved in every way, that she should be respectful toward her parents-in-law, and that this is the will of *Chau*. They tell her that *Chau* gave her to her parents, and that they are now giving her away to this man. The man was given good advice by his parents before they left his home to fetch the girl. If parents are too young to give advice, they find an old person to give it, like the old woman we took along one time or someone else who is an effective speaker, maybe a grandparent.

100

During all this time the groom has stayed at a distance. The bride has listened to all that has been said, but has not spoken a word; it is our custom that she, on this occasion, says nothing to anyone. Others do the talking.

"It has happened that the girl is so totally surprised that she is being given away in marriage that she expresses resentment and refuses to leave her home. In fact, she may, without saying a word, dash out of the *ruka* and be on her way if the formation of the assisting men is carelessly formed. I have seen such a woman get away; we saw her running over fields and hills like a rabbit. When this happens, the men who came with the man's father and who should have been on the alert chase after the girl—all thirty of them, if there are that many. It is their duty to see that she is brought back, for she must go with the young man. The men got on their horses in this instance and galloped after this reluctant bride; in fact, I lent one of them my horse. They caught her and brought her back, and she had to go with the man. She is still living with him, and I believe they are happy—at least they seem to be. The four women whom I helped to get were willing to go with the men, but I did see this one run away, the one I just told you about. She ran like a rabbit!" He was still amused by it.

Huenun went on to say that if the woman makes no resistance and all has proceeded properly, she is told to sit where she can see the customary presents being given to her parents by the man's relatives. Her mother may be given silver hair ornaments, silver jewelry, and maybe a *chamall* which she is to use as clothing for herself.

After the gifts have been presented, the man comes closer to the *ruka*. A sheep that was brought by his father as part of the bride price is now slaughtered, prepared as food, and served as a meal to the young woman and her family. All of the sheep must be eaten, including its blood, all except the bones—which are thrown into a river or lake to make certain that no dog will get them. "If dogs eat any of that sheep, even the bones, ill luck will come to both families," Huenun said with certainty. After the bride's family has eaten, they slaughter a sheep and serve it to all persons present. This sheep is not considered sacred in any way; only the one that is fed to the woman's family is.

Although the groom joins the crowd while the meal is being prepared, he and the bride do not talk to each other until after the two meals. It is then that he comes to her. They now take each other's hands. "This is not like taking each other's hands during the ceremony in the churches today," said Huenun. "Generally, no one present even notices it. Now, this is really the first time these two are near each other. Very, very rarely, formerly, did the man and woman face each other before this occasion. Older persons present now tell them to love each other, to establish a family, and to live a good family life together." The woman is lifted on a horse, and she and the man ride to the latter's paternal *ruka*. Here they are now at home.

They will be at home in a section of this *ruka* for several years probably, after which a *ruka* will be erected for them. Should it happen that the woman is needed in her father's house—maybe because her mother is not well and is unable to do her work—the couple will make their home in the woman's paternal *ruka*. "But this is a rare thing. Pride of the *Mapuches* will not permit a man to live in the *ruka* that was his wife's home," said Huenun.

After the woman has lived with her husband for some time, she goes to her own home to fetch animals that were hers, also blankets she wove, and whatever else she had accumulated through her own efforts. She will also bring back whatever her parents and relatives give her. If she herself does not fetch these things, they will be sent to her by her parents, if her father so decides. If her father is a rich man, he may give her several horses, several head of cattle, and some sheep in addition to her own property; possibly, also, he might give her some silver ornaments. If he is a poor man, she will receive very little from him.

"When I was about thirty years old," he continued, "my uncles talked to me about getting married. Since I had no father, they took it upon themselves to find a woman for me, but I preferred to go to

Argentina with one uncle. I wanted to try my skill at rounding up wild cattle, of which there were many on the pampa. Then, too, I was too poor to get married." He laughed about this. "One moon came, and another passed, then another, and then more time passed. My uncles urged me to consent to marry the woman they had found for me, the one I am now married to; they said she would make a good wife for me. They kept telling me not to go to Argentina, because too many men who went there settled down and never returned; they did not want me to do likewise.

"One of my uncles finally talked to the woman's father; these two agreed that two horses would be sufficient for the bride price. That was taking the only horse I owned, and since I needed two, my aunt gave me one of hers. Some weeks later we went for the woman: three old men, six young men, and five or six women. Among these were my uncles and my aunt—all of them were relatives. From my own earnings, I bought another horse soon after we were married, but this one I had to use as pay for the *machitun* that I told you about a few days ago. My wife, too, was poor; all she owned were two cows. She brought the cows with her, but a puma killed both. Later we acquired three horses, and I traded one of these for a cow, and from this cow we now have the twenty-four cattle we own. We now, also, own six horses—everyone in the family owns a horse. And, I believe, we have twenty-three sheep.

"I do not think my wife knew that I was going to marry her. I have never talked to her about it, and I do not think I ever will. We love each other, and we have always done so, and that is what is important. I would not offend her by asking her that question. I had never spoken to my wife before we were married, for as I told you, it is one of our customs that a man and the woman he intends to marry will not talk to each other before marriage. They will, yes, if they have an opportunity to do so secretly, but there is seldom such an opportunity. I had no opportunity to talk to my wife before our marriage, and then, too, I hesitated to talk to her because I was poor. Although she was poor, she was richer than I was. I would like to have talked to her though, for it is only human that when one is in love, he wants to talk to the one he loves. Two or three months before we were married, I talked to her father, and she may then have suspected something, but I never talked to her, as I said. I am generally liked by people. I do not offend anyone, and I do not hurt anyone. There were no objections raised when my uncle asked for her.

"My wife was well bred. She was chaste, too; she had been well guarded by her mother. In general, girls were chaste before their marriage, and they are so today. In good families it is impossible for a girl to meet men before marriage; in bad families, yes, such things happen. If a *Mapuche* gets a girl pregnant with a promise of marriage and then does not keep his word, her brothers will see that the spirit of evil is put into him and in that way have his mind taken from him. Such a retaliation we call *wulla*. Once in a while, too, there is a woman who goes around and lives with many men and is not married to any man, but there are very few of these. It is our custom that a man marry several women, but never is a woman to marry more than one man."

When I asked him if wife-lending was an early Araucanian custom, saying that there is reference to it in travelers' literature, he replied, "I have never heard of anyone lending his wife to another *Mapuche* or to a visitor among the *Mapuches* or to anyone else." When asked about a man lending a daughter to a visitor—such reference is also found—his whole demeanor and facial expression seemed to repel the idea, and he said with indignation and most emphatically, "Much less that! Some of those *huincas* think they know something about the *Mapuches* and then write such stuff to lessen the *Mapuches* in the eyes of others. I got around much as a young man. I saw and heard much, but I never met up with anything like that. I cannot recall ever even having heard of it.

"It happened formerly, and occasionally happens today, that a man who already has one wife, or maybe several, sees another girl whom he likes and then sends a group of men to kidnap her. Kidnaping is done at night. The girl may struggle and her father may object and everybody will yell at everybody, but no one can prevent the girl from being taken; her family is outnumbered by strong men.

"Our marriage customs have changed. I know that paying the bride price is a problem today: old people want it paid; young people ignore it. Today, it happens, too, that a girl will go to the home of the man she likes. If the man likes her also, she is usually allowed to stay at his home, that is, if his father permits it. Formerly, no father of any man would have allowed it. I myself think it is all right to permit it today, provided the man and the woman truly love each other. I am convinced that we can no longer keep our old customs in the matter of marriage, and I have no intention of arranging the marriage of my daughter Teresa, who is now twenty years old. I have sent my daughters to school to learn to read and write, and they should be able to exercise some judgment. Up in the Cordillera and out on the *campo* you will find parents who do not yet send their daughters to school. In such families, the father of the man and the father of the girl decide on the animals that are to be paid for the girl, and then when these are paid, the girl must go with the man whether she wants to or not. It is a remnant of the custom I just told you about. In such groups of *Mapuches* the girl may not choose her husband. In these families girls usually learn only what all *Mapuche* women must learn, namely, to care for a household; they learn no more than that."

At this point I thought it opportune to ask questions to verify and to clarify information that we had collected on the coastal range which dealt with preferential marriage, marriage prohibitions, joking, and in-law relationships. I did so. He flared up and, in a tone of voice that left no doubt that his temper had been aroused, said, "I have been told that you asked these same questions of *Mapuches* on the Pacific coast. Do you not believe what they have told you? Do you ask every *Mapuche* the same questions?" I put on an air of dignified vexation and explained that I, at times, wanted information on a topic from several persons, because customs sometimes differed from one group to another among a people, and that it was for this reason that I was asking him for information on these particular items. Had he not told me that there were dialect variations in the *Mapuches* language? And was it not possible that there might be variations in other things, too? I asked.

Having given vent to his resentment and, I believe, having thereby kept his ego inflated, he snorted, "Are you ready now to listen? Is *Señorita* Margarita ready to write things down? If so, let us begin!"

Margaret thought he might as well have commanded, "Ready? One, two, three—go!"

He began, but he talked at a slow pace, halting patiently after each phrase or sentence. He rested his eyes on Margaret's notebook and continued only after she had written what he had said, a slow procedure which was particularly helpful in this case. "My son can marry my sister's daughter [that was the first sentence]. My daughter can marry my sister's son [that was his second sentence]. In other words, my children can marry my sister's children [that was his third sentence, a summary statement]. Also, my son can marry the daughter of my wife's brother; my daughter can marry the son of my wife's brother. In other words, my children can marry the children of my wife's brother. On the contrary, my son cannot marry my brother's daughter, nor can my daughter marry my brother's son; in other words, my children cannot marry my brother's children. Also, my son cannot marry the daughter of my wife's sister, nor can my daughter marry the son of my wife's sister; in other words, my children cannot marry the children of my wife's sister. The children of two sisters cannot marry each other any more than the children of two brothers can." I had now verified what we had learned on the coastal range: Araucanians may marry cross-cousins; they may not marry parallel cousins.

With great exactness Margaret had written down each bit of information, and at the end she passed me a slip of paper on which she had written, "I hope this is clearer than mud!"

"It is crystal clear." I answered.

Huenun continued: "Where there are two or more wives, the children of them cannot marry each other, even though the wives are not blood relatives; these children are considered brothers and

106

sisters because they both have the same father. But if a man's second wife—not a sister to his first wife—has brothers and sisters and they have children, the man's children by his first wife can marry the children of the brothers and sisters of his second wife, for relatives of a wife of my father, a wife who is not my mother, are no relatives of mine; I can marry them as I like. Now, a thing that has been done, but is not our custom nor is it liked by the people when it is done, is that a man marry his father's widow; that is, one who was a wife of his father but not the woman who bore him. A man lived here whose father died, leaving a young wife. The man's son by another wife then lived with this young wife as though married to her, and the people talked about this, for it is not our custom. Also, under no condition can a man marry his father's mother or his mother's mother: these both stand in very high regard with reference to a child. Neither can a woman ever marry her mother's father nor her father's father. No, never! Of all things, that least of all!

"And now with regard to relatives with whom I may joke," he continued. "I may joke with my wife's sisters who are younger than my wife, but not with those who are older than my wife, for I must respect them. My wife can joke with my brothers who are younger than I, but not with brothers older than I, for she must respect them. These are our customs. Women can joke among themselves and talk about anything they like, and men can do the same among themselves; but a man talks to no woman except his wife and her younger sisters, unless it is absolutely necessary. A wife talks to no man, unless it is necessary, except her husband, his younger brothers, such in-laws as her own sister's husband, and the man married to her husband's sister. However, she is not to joke with these men; she may joke only with her husband's younger brothers. It is necessary for a woman to talk to other men only when her husband is not at home, and aside from this she has nothing to say when men are present. A *Mapuche* greatly dislikes to see his wife talking to a man who is not a relative. Formerly, if a man suspected his wife of casting eyes on another man, he made certain that she was doing so, and then he cut off one of her braids. By this act everybody knew of her offense, and she was embarrassed. He would treat her badly, too, even whip her."

"I know now, Huenun," I said, "that what we learned on the coastal range was correct; it agrees with what you have just told us. Can you tell us more about in-laws?"

"A man has great respect for his father-in-law," he replied. "A man, when he arrives at the house of his father-in-law, must conduct with him the *koyaqtun* in a special way—it is much like the regular *koyaqtun*, except that it is carried on in a monotonous rise and fall of pitch. The father-in-law begins, 'How are you? How is your wife?' and so on, asking about everyone in the son-in-law's *ruka*. Then the son-in-law asks the same questions of his father-in-law in the same singsong tone. All questions are answered on both sides. Then they ask each other about more distant relatives, always in a rhythmic tone. They continue this until the father-in-law says it is enough. This must be done at every visit."

Huenun stepped to the window to take a look at the position of the sun. "How can you tell time at night?" I asked him.

"Who wants to know the time at night? he answered. "There is no sense to that. Direction, yes; a person needs to know how to get home at night. If the stars are out, he can let them lead him; if not, he must stay overnight in someone's *ruka*. He can either find *pünon*, the Footprint of Rhea; or *l'uan*, the Guanaco; or *lükai*, the Boleodora; or *utrul poñü*, Pile of Potatoes; or *yépún*, the Evening Star; or *wünyelfe*, the Morning Star," He pointed at the locations of these constellations as he mentioned them. Astronomically, it seems, *pünon* is Reticulum; *utrul poñü*, a star in Pavo; *lükai*, one in Crux; and *l'uan*, in Centaurus.

"And now it is time for me to set out for home," he noted. He again invited us to his home. "You must come to my *ruka* before you leave Panguipulli," he said, tapping the window sill for emphasis.

"We shall come, Huenun, the day after tomorrow," I assured him. "Can you come to show us the way?"

108

"Can you be here about the time that the sun is there [zenith]?" asked Huenun. "I shall be here. My wife will be glad to know that you are coming."

We presented him with a sack of flour, shook hands warmly, sent greetings to his wife and family, and walked with him to where his horse was grazing. We watched him unhobble and mount it. He waved good-bye to us and the children and workmen in the yard, and galloped away.

Margaret and I set out for a relaxing walk. Our favorite stroll in Panguipulli was through a pasture, over and under fences, to a spot on a hillside from which we could view the sunset on the white snowy tops of four mighty and impressive volcanoes: Shoshuenco, a mighty warrior, according to Huenun; Quetropillán, a stranger to us; Villarrica, a beauty in symmetry; and Lanín, stately and tallest of all. The last rays of the sun on their hoods of snow reflected the colors of the rainbow, then faded into each other blending into a hue of tender blue, and out into the blue of steel. As the sun set on these mountaintops, it was as though another day was saying good night to Shoshuenco first, then to Quetropillán, next to Villarrica, and lastly to Lanín. The valleys, until now but half-revealed, became dark as night, and soon the Cordillera was silhouetted against the sunset sky. Another day had passed into eternal time. As we sat there in silence, I recited to Margaret a couplet that I had learned from a scrap of paper which I had picked up while among the Piegans and the Blood Indians in the stupendous Canadian Rockies—the composer's name was not given: *"The peace of God is a most profound tranquillity and repose, Like the silence of untrodden mountain summits clothed in eternal snows."*

Dusk was upon us. Margaret and I trailed home, tranquil and refreshed, our souls at peace with God and man.

CHAPTER X

Adiós, *Huenun!* Adiós!

Huenun arrived before the sun was at its zenith. Since it had looked as though it would shower, he had started from home early. He looked about the room and walked over to our bags and boxes and typewriter, which were packed and ready for our trip to higher valleys in the Andes. He seemed pensive. "Now that you must leave, I know what your friendship has meant to me," he said sadly. I remarked that I was certain that he had had good friends before we met him and that these would continue to be his friends after we had left. He pulled a chair up to the table, and so did Margaret and I. His face radiated that kindly expression we had seen the day he had brought his wife and daughter. "Father Sigifredo," he began, "has been the best friend that I have had in my lifetime; he has been like a father to me. Yes, Father Sigifredo has been my best friend." He sat there for a while, looking into space, visibly moved. With his fist he brushed tears off his cheeks and continued, "Sincere and true friends of all *Mapuches* are the wild animals, and every *Mapuche* is a friend of all animals. That animals are the *Mapuches'* friends has often been proven. For example, it is known that a *Mapuche* had ridden his horse several days, one time, before he came upon food. He prayed to *Chau* to send him food, and before long a puma brought a small animal that it had killed. It laid the animal at the feet of that man's horse, then left, and went far away—it did this to allow the *Mapuche* to dismount and eat without fear."

110

Francisca announced that our midday meal was ready. After eating, we packed food to take with us; we expected to eat our evening meal at Huenun's home. In all probability it would be dusk before we returned to the mission. Huenun, Francisca, Margaret, and I started out, following an oxcart trail. "On horseback it takes me twenty minutes to go home," he said; "on foot it will take a longer time, of course." Later, he remarked, "At the slow pace you are going, it will take us an hour to get to my *ruka*. I should have borrowed horses so that you could have ridden." We had expressed a preference to walk when, on the previous day, he had offered to bring us horses to ride.

We sauntered along the trail for some time, then followed a footpath that cut across fields and another that wound around a meadow. We followed pathways that led through brush and bushes, meadows and fields, and occasionally we skirted a *ruka* and its gardens. We passed close to a Chilean homestead where a woman sat doing some work. "With your permission, *señora*," said Huenun standing still for a moment. We, too, asked permission, bowed, and walked on. We crawled under and over fences. There were fences of rails that rested in openings cut into posts; fences of split tree-trunks set upright and close together; fences of saplings tied to posts with stout vines; fences of burnt-down tree-trunks piled helter-skelter. I remarked that one had to perform acrobatic stunts to get over or under or through these fences. Huenun laughed heartily. "These fences?" he questioned. "These fences keep grazing animals from wandering into other people's fields." Occasionally, we stopped to eat luscious blackberries—thousands of them hung on tall bushes, glistening with raindrops of the morning's shower. Huenun resented them and would not eat any.

Francisca remarked, "Every inhabitant in this part of Chile considers these blackberries a pest. Everybody blames everybody else for introducing them. The Germans blame the French for bringing the first ones into Chile; the French blame the Germans for doing so; both Germans and French are blamed by Araucanians and Chileans for introducing them. What is known for certain is

111

that they were introduced by European settlers who planted them to serve as enclosures for sheep. When the brambles grew beyond control, goats were introduced to eat the brambles. Grain fields that were free of all pests only three years ago are now overrun with blackberry brambles. No one can tell how it will all end."

Huenun now led us to the top of a knoll to view the scenery. He pointed out the beauties of this valley: in the distance stood the majestic, impressive Andean ranges; directly in front of us lay the quiet waters of Lake Panguipulli; to our left, in all his majesty, stood symmetrical Volcano Villarrica, puffing away sporadically. Huenun remarked that he puffed with pride and that he was doing so from the depths of the earth. Then there was Shoshuenco; it was he who in a quarrel with Villarrica blew out his top and died. "No one has seen him puff since," said Huenun, "but he wants Villarrica to know that he is not devoid of all pride; that is why he wears his hat [cloud formations that appeared like a broad-brimmed hat]. See with what dignity he wears it? But, as I told you some days ago, we have learned in recent years that Villarrica cannot be trusted; he may start up at any time to throw rocks of brimstone, and who knows for how long. I fear he has turned out to be a treacherous, untrustworthy fellow. Then over there," he continued, "almost on top of the Cordillera is Lanín. He wears a hat at all times. The Argentines claim him, but he is respected on both sides of the Cordillera." We continued to walk.

"Were you born in this valley?" I asked.

"No, I was not," he answered; "but my wife was. I was born in Chinquil, near Melefquen. One can still see a grove of apple trees where we then lived; I know where the place is. I have heard it said that we had so many apples that we made large vats of chicha each year. We lived there with my father's father while I was still small, for my father was poor. He went to Concepción to defend his rights to his land and lay claim to it. Later we heard that he had gone to Valdivia. We have always thought that he had no money with which to come back and that probably he married another woman there; we never heard from him again. I have often wondered if he is still living. His name was Kalfuñamku, which means 'Blue-eagle'; my mother's name was Kalfukar, as I told you before. I had a younger brother who was known by his baptismal name, José Miguel.

"When I was a little older we moved to Anacomoi—we had to leave Chinquil for it was impossible to live there any longer; *fundo* owners, both Chileans and those from other countries, were robbing us of our land; they were moving in upon us everywhere. My grandparents were buried in Anacomoi; so was my mother. The place is now a *fundo*, and their burial place is a wheat field, but I know where their graves are. I recall well how these intruding *fundo* people planted oats right up to the yard of our *ruka*. When the ears appeared on the stalks, I knew the stalks were ready to be made into fifes. So, I took some stalks and made fifes of them. The *inquilino* heard me play these, and because of it, he harangued my mother and grandmother. My mother advised me not to fife again, and I never again did. With nothing to do, I began to catch swallows in a trap that I had made.

"This reminds me that I forgot to tell you about this type of trap. Well, I made a trap by poking a little stick into the earth and fastening to it a slipknot of horsehair which served as a noose. On the opposite side of the stick, I stuck a goose feather in the ground, and then I lay nearby to watch a swallow come to get the goose feather for her nest. In order to get it, she had to stand in the noose and reach for it. Moving around doing this caused the noose to close in on her legs, and so she was caught. With wings outspread, she struggled to get away. When I caught my first swallow, I was greatly pleased, and I took it to my grandmother. She tied a cord to one of its legs to keep it from flying away and told me to tame it. But just then along came a woman who bought it from me; she paid me four potatoes for it.

"And then came sad days. My younger brother, José Miguel, took sick; someone had used witchcraft on him. Herbal decoctions that my father's sister gave him did not help; he spat blood, and soon he dried up and died. Two years later my mother died; witch-

113

craft had been exercised on her, too; we suspected a relative had done this to both my brother and my mother. And so I became an orphan. My grandparents cared for me, and I helped them when I could; I always fetched wood and water for them. I remember my grandmother weaving *chamall* with which to clothe me. When I had no work to do, I made toys. Once I made a miniature yoke, a wooden plow, and a pole used in leading oxen. I yoked two cats to the plow by tying the yoke to their ears. Elders teased me about it, but I had fun doing it. I also carved horses of wood so their heads had ears and a mouth, which I then bridled with ropes made from shreds of bark.

"Then my grandfather died. I was old enough by then to go into our fields to keep parrots from eating seeds planted there. Even today flocks of parrots that pass through our valley soon after the fields are freshly sown feed on the seeds; they are on their way to higher mountains. I was happy out in the fields and sang our songs, but when I came home, I would become sad for I would think of my grandfather and cry. My grandmother would comfort me, then; but she, too, would weep. I remember it was at this time that a son of my father's brother went far away; they said he had gone to clear land by burning down woods. When I was older, I left the home of my grandmother to find work on a *fundo*. I was probably twenty years old when I returned home. Here I found that one of my relatives, more than thirty years old, had returned from a school in Valdivia where he had learned to read and write—he is the one who taught me to read and to write, as I told you."

We turned into a narrow rut now and walked in goose fashion. As soon as we reached the end of it, Huenun continued: "We are not far from my *ruka* now. The land we own, thirty hectares [approximately seventy-five acres], was given my wife by her father, as I told you before. Much of it is wet land and can be used only for grazing. It is good grazing land, however; the grass is green all the year around. I would like to drain it and grow grain in it, but that is impossible. There are fine trees on it too: *canelo* [*Drimys*

114

winteri], *temu* [*Temu divaricatum*], and *patagua* [*Myrceugenia planipes*].

"In addition to our land, we have three pairs of oxen. When they were still calves, I gave them to my sons, who were then little boys, and so the oxen belong to them."

"What are the names of the oxen?" I asked.

"Their names?" and he laughed. "Well, Jerónimo's are called *Tesoro* [treasure] and *Madrugada* [early riser]. Juan has two pairs. One pair is called *Pajarito* [little bird] and his partner, *Valiente* [valiant]. Since Valiente moved straight forward while he was being trained and seemed like a valiant man, he was given that name. Juan's other pair is *Alegre* [lively] and *Talamera* [bird snare].

"We also own five cows. I called one *Cordillera*, because she is speckled like some volcanoes on which snow shows up white, and forests, dark. Then there are *Cabra* [goat], *Rosada* [frost-colored], *Clavel* [carnation], and I have forgotten the names of the others. Sheep have no names. We have a flock of thirty-seven: twenty are mine, and seventeen belong to relatives. These seventeen I pasture *in media*, that is, I get half of the lambs they bear; the relatives get the other half.

"I own three horses. The one I ride—you have seen it every time I have come to help you—I named *Calzado*, because he has white feet and white ankles. *Chercana* is named for the bird chercan, because it has the color of that bird. I just bought a third horse, but I do not know by what name it is called. I had another horse, but the other day I gave it to the herbalist for the remedies and the treatment she gave Jerónimo. Since I did not have any money, she said she would accept a horse."

"Tell us about your children," I said.

"My children? Well, Juan Venicio is my eldest son; he is thirty years old," replied Huenun. "Eventually he will marry, but he says his time to marry has not yet come. He cultivates land he has rented from a Chilean. Then comes Fabian, twenty-eight years old. He studied to be a chauffeur, but he has had no opportunity to be one.

115

He is mechanically minded and likes his work as a blacksmith on a *fundo* owned by a company not far from Osorno. He wrote to Jerónimo that he is married, but he did not write me—probably because he thought I would be angry with him. I have no objections to marriage; in the end he would have to marry anyway. We do not know whether he married a *Mapuche* or a Chilean—many Chileans live near Osorno. He once told me of a dream he had: he dreamed he had married a fine-looking girl, but did not know from where she came; in his dream he was not living at home when he married. Then comes Rosalia; she is now twenty-six years old. She was with the sisters at school for two years, and I would have sent her to school longer, but she had to help at home. We had a boy born with a cleft palate who had to be fed a drop at a time; this required much time. The little boy died when he was two years old, and after that Rosalia lived as a servant girl in the house of a *fundo* owner. The wife on the *fundo* and her husband often went away from home and left all the household in Rosalia's care; they trusted her. Jerónimo came next; he is twenty-five years old now. He has not been well since he returned from military service, where he was badly treated by the officer in charge.

"Our next child is Atanaseo; he is twenty-three years old. He is still at home with us. Today he is helping his brother on his [the brother's] rented land; on other days he helps me. And then our last child is Teresa, twenty years old, who is also still with us. Today she is helping her brothers and will not be at home. Five girls and two boys born to us have died."

He now pointed out *rukas*, here and there and over there, and said there were eleven of them, that *Mapuche* families lived in all of them, and that all were related to each other and to him—some on his father's side, some on his mother's side. We had learned on the coastal range that the Araucanians have no villages but live on homesteads not too far from each other. Later we found this to be true in the higher valleys, also.

As we approached his homestead, we passed through a sparse-

116

ly productive wheat field. "This is the field that I told you is bewitched," he said. "You can see for yourself the many weeds in it and the blackberry brambles. The harvest was so poor that we plucked the ears by hand. We always harvest a small field by hand, but this field is large and should have required a sickle to cut it. I took the ears of wheat to a threshing machine—a Chilean brings one around here at harvest time. The Chilean charged two kilos for every sack threshed—a sack holds fifty kilos. After paying him, I had sixteen sacks left, and of these I had to give eight to another Chilean who had given me the seed at planting time last spring—I had agreed to raise the wheat on my land and give him half."

Peas were ready to be harvested, and of these he expected a good supply. "Tomorrow I shall cut the vines, and on one of the following days, when a pair of oxen will be here, I shall haul them home—the oxen are now being used by one of my sons. This year's crop of peas is so large that we need one or two horses to thresh it. Horses do this by stamping the vines in a *lila* in the same way as we formerly threshed grain. I told you about this one day. If the crop of peas was small, we would beat the vines with sticks. And here is the plow that I made from a tree trunk; it is drawn by two oxen when we plow our fields. This is the sickle I use for cutting grain." He had made the sickle by securely tying a blade of metal to a sapling which served as a handle.

We had now entered the gate of his yard. His wife was approaching to bid us welcome. We were glad to see each other again. At her heels came hippety-hoppeting Rosamella, their three-year-old granddaughter, and after her came Jerónimo and Hortensia, the twelve-year-old daughter of Huenun's niece—the niece had died when Hortensia was small. Huenun introduced them with an affectionate glance at each. We all greeted each other with warm handshakes, and then Huenun led us to see the loom on which his wife was weaving *chamall*; it was to be used as a *küpam*, that is, as a dress, for herself. Both warp and woof were finely spun yarn of natural, black wool; she needed more as woof. "If I do not get more

117

black wool soon," she said, "I shall need to dye white wool with black German dye—we call the German dyes *anül*—but I prefer the sheep's own dye of black."

Huenun next wanted us to see his two *rukas*—two frame houses patterned after the traditional thatched *ruka*. The framework of each was of scantlings; walls and roof were slabs; all had been obtained at a lumber mill in the Cordillera. Each *ruka* had a door of planks and a window opening covered either with slats or with a hanging of gunnysack. One ruka, consisting of only a single room, was kitchen and eating place. Smoke drifted through both protruding gable ends and in places in the walls where slabs had been omitted for this purpose. In a pit in the floor, about the middle of the *ruka*, a fire was smoldering, and over it hung kettles, suspended by iron chains from a rod fastened to opposite walls. Hooks at the ends of the chains held the kettles securely. At various places of the framework, sections of *colihüe* stalks were fastened, and from them hung braids of onions, twigs of medicinal plants, a sheep pelt on a stretcher, bunches of corn, several baskets, a winnowing tray, and other household supplies. Furnishings consisted of a chair, several low benches, a table, and a small cabinet with dishes and bowls containing food. In a corner of the *ruka* lay a heap of potatoes.

The other *ruka*, a two-room structure, was used for sleeping and storage. As we entered it, we found Maríañuke's mother and Lauriana, Maríañuke's sister, resting against sacks of grain. The mother, Huenun said, was more than one hundred years old; Lauriana had come to visit the mother and had stayed on. "We asked her to stay here," said Huenun. "She had nothing more to eat at home."

When we were back in the yard, Huenun suggested that everyone get ready to have pictures taken. We might forget to take them later; besides, shadows would soon interfere with good photography. He told his wife to wear her silver ornaments. Jerónimo sent Hortensia for his coat. Rosamella fetched Maríañuke's mother and Lauriana. After Huenun had placed everyone so that there would be ample sunlight on all, I took the photographs. All seemed partic-

118

ularly glad to have Maríañuke's mother photographed. I promised to send Huenun a copy of each, and did so.

Huenun, his wife, and Jerónimo then took us to see the rest of the homestead. "These are chestnut trees," said Huenun. "When I was helping Father Félix José with the *Diccionarios*, we went to Valdivia. The chestnuts were ripe then, and I brought several home. I planted them, and they produced these shade trees. Here are our turkeys, twelve of them. We also have thirty chickens and eleven geese."

Since he seemed particularly fond of the geese—he cackled and talked to them—I took a picture of him standing near them. His wife was amused and said to him, "So, now you have had your picture taken with geese!" Huenun called attention to shelters: straw and hay were stored in a tall, drafty one; a low, closely built one sheltered fowl at night.

We came to the well. "This well is six meters deep; its water is cool and clear and clean," Huenun remarked. "We surmised that water was here, for in winter water always seeped to the surface. Formerly, we took our water from a spring close to the *ruka*, but the spring was only one meter deep."

Just then Hortensia brought a bucket and drew water. Seeing her do so made me think that Maríañuke might like to have a picture of herself drawing water. She was pleased. I said that maybe she would want to remove her silver ornaments so that she would look as though she were working. In a friendly manner she replied, "Most certainly! Quite obviously no one would work with those things on!" I asked her if she would mind posing once more so I could photograph her with the bucket just as it was coming from the well—the one I had taken showed her emptying the bucket into a wooden container. She did not seem pleased about this, but did so after throwing a meaningful glance at Huenun and saying something to him in Araucanian.

Margaret said to me, "This probably falls into the category of repeating something."

We walked on leisurely and arrived at the orchard. "These are

119

four wild apple trees; their apples make better chicha than do these orchard apples. And these trees bear sweet cherries; those trees bear sour ones. We seldom harvest sour cherries; the birds eat them as fast as they ripen—they seem to enjoy them. People come here to buy our sweet cherries. Here are plum trees and pear trees. Fruit that falls to the ground our two pigs enjoy." Maríañuke added, "Apples and plums we cut in halves and dry on racks over the fireplace for winter use. Before we eat them, we wash them well in hot water to get rid of the taste of smoke. But from most of our apples we make chicha, and also from the pears of one tree; the pears of another tree we eat or sell. We fill three barrels with chicha each year; together they hold 360 liters."

Maríañuke left for the *ruka*. Francisca accompanied her. I asked Huenun, "What seasons have you here in Panguipulli?"

"There are seven," he answered. "The year begins when the days begin to be longer than the nights. The span of time from then until it is time to plant, we call *wetripantu*—it is time to plant wheat when leaf buds of the roble chileno [*Nothofagus obliqua*] are as large as the kernels on that cob of corn [pointing at one]. We plant corn when the vine we call *paulum* [*Hydrangea integerrima*] has buds. When the things we have planted show growth, we say '*Wün'ntripantu* is here.' After that comes *antütripantu*, summer—some call it *antügnen*. Then comes the time when there is an abundance to eat, all the harvest is ripe; it is called *monmapu* [fertile earth]. We are having *monmapu* now. Next comes *chomügnen*, and after that the forerunner of winter, *konmepukem*. And then follows *pukem*, winter."

He pointed to his garden: "It does not amount to much; only the cabbage has matured. The potatoes and all other plants whose roots we eat have not developed. It is as I told you: someone has done damage to my land through witchcraft. This corn field has produced, but not enough so that we shall have corn for winter use. We usually put up a winter's supply of peas, corn, and potatoes."

"Do you store meat for winter use?" I asked.

"Why should that be done? Our sheep and fowl are always

with us. My wife decides what meat she wants for the day, and we see that she has it: sometimes we kill fowl, then; sometimes a large animal. Of a large animal there is usually meat left over from which she makes *charqui* [jerked meat]. Old people have told us that before the Spaniards came, we ate meat of guanaco and rhea; there were plenty of these animals in our country then."

We walked on. "Here is a *ñocha* [*Greigia landbeckii*]," he noted. "The rope my wife used in drawing water from the well was one I made from strands of this *ñocha. Ñocha* blades are pulled out by the roots and passed back and forth through a fire to soften them. Soft ones are easily pulled apart into strands. The number of strands to use depends on the thickness you want the rope to be."

Just then he saw a fungus on a tree. "Here! See here! This is the kind on which I learned to write," he said gleefully, and removed it from the tree trunk. He suggested that I photograph him. "I will use this twig and pose as though I were writing."

We were back at the *ruka*, impressed by the cleanliness of everything and everybody, as we had been with every Araucanian household and person we had seen anywhere. Whether we came upon a family unexpectedly or not, always all was clean. Fences that protected fields and orchards and gardens from hungry and aggressive animals gave one a feeling, too, that order prevailed.

Francisca came to tell us it was getting late. She had planned to arrange our evening meal so we could all enjoy it together, but Maríañuke insisted that her house was not good enough, that she would set a table for us in the open, and that we should eat there while she prepared a meal for her household. A table was therefore set for Margaret, Francisca, and me under one of the chestnut trees, with a chair or box for each of us. Margaret filled our little teapot with water from the well, hung it over the fireplace in the *ruka*, and while waiting for it to boil played with Rosamella. Here at Huenun's, there was no need for her to keep an eye on the teapot. It was Margaret's "holy" duty to keep this little teapot in her possession at all times, and to see that the water for our beverage was boiled in it and in no other. It was she herself who filled it with

121

water from the well or spring, and who kept an eye on it until it boiled, when she removed it to make our beverage. Although we trusted everyone, we had been warned by non-Araucanians and by Araucanians themselves that an unfriendly person might put poison into our food or beverage. We took no chances!

Francisca had unpacked our evening meal, and we offered a goodly portion of it to Maríañuke for her family—we had packed it with the thought of sharing it with them. Rosamella got an extra sandwich from Margaret. Huenun looked at her until she thanked Margaret in both Spanish and Araucanian, and then told her to sit down to eat it and not to disturb us until we had finished our meal. She did just this. Huenun asked if we would accept some cheese— his wife had made it and wanted us to have some. We did, and found it perfect. Francisca interpolated that cheese making was learned at the Mission School.

After we had eaten, everyone came forward, and we bade each other farewell. We again expressed sincere appreciation for the courtesies that had been shown us, and again thanked Huenun for his help. I believed him to be one of the finest aborigines of the Americas that I had met. We thanked Maríañuke, our gracious hostess. To her mother and sister we offered warm handclasps, and farewells for Hortensia, Jerónimo, and spritely, lovable, little Rosamella, with greetings left for those of the household not at home.

As we approached the gate, Huenun took from his coat pocket a note, handed it to me, and said, "I wrote this note, but the sentiments expressed in it are my wife's; she asked me to write it."

It read: "I am most grateful to the North American sister because she came to my house to see me, and because she took a photograph of my ordinary house and of my poor mother, who is also thankful and who is always here with me."

I put an envelope into Huenun's hand, and we parted. The envelope contained some pesos and a note which read: "These pesos, Huenun, will buy you fertilizer for all your fields. We, too, want you to have another abundant crop of grain. With all our hearts we wish you God's blessings."

Our days at Panguipulli had come to an end. At dawn the next morning we were on a lumber-hauling *vapór* on the shores of Lake Panguipulli, en route to Coñaripe. Francisca went with us—a joy to both her and us. We were to sail across Lakes Panguipulli and Calefquén, and then journey up the Andes by truck and oxcart to Coñaripe Valley. We should like to have called to Huenun once again, "*Adiós*, Huenun! *Adiós!*"

Index

127